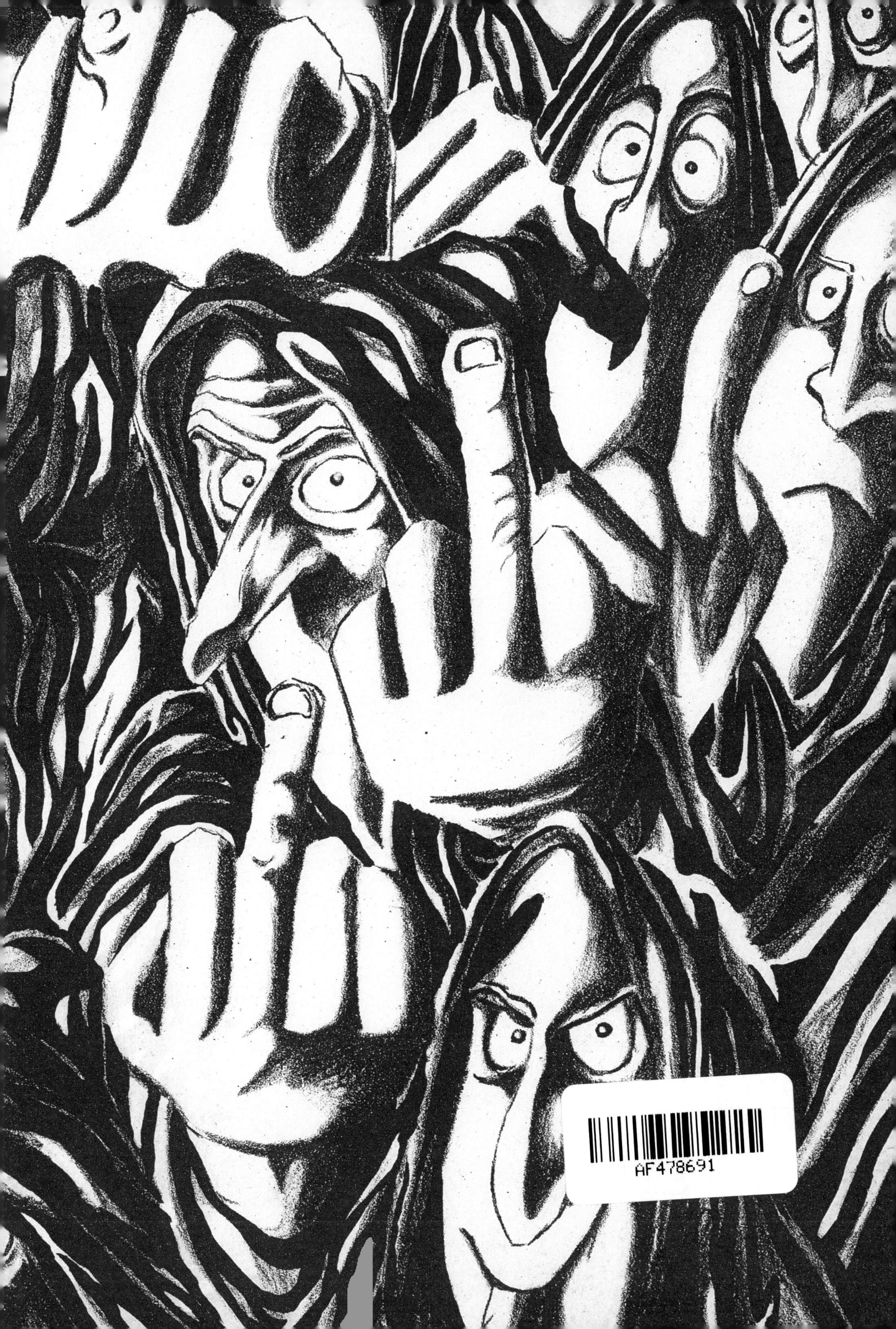
AF478691

Martin Bigum

The Face of God

jrp | ringier

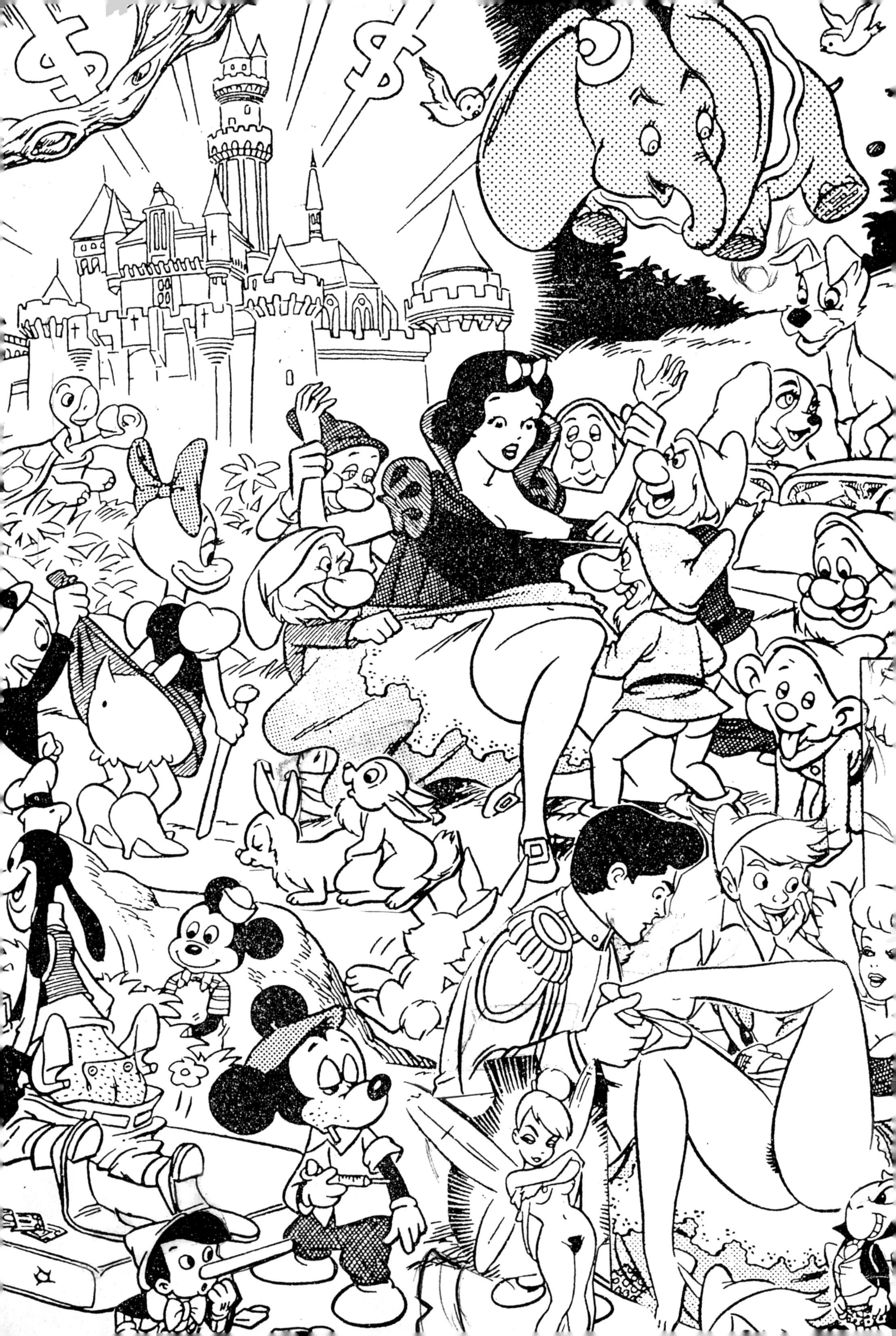

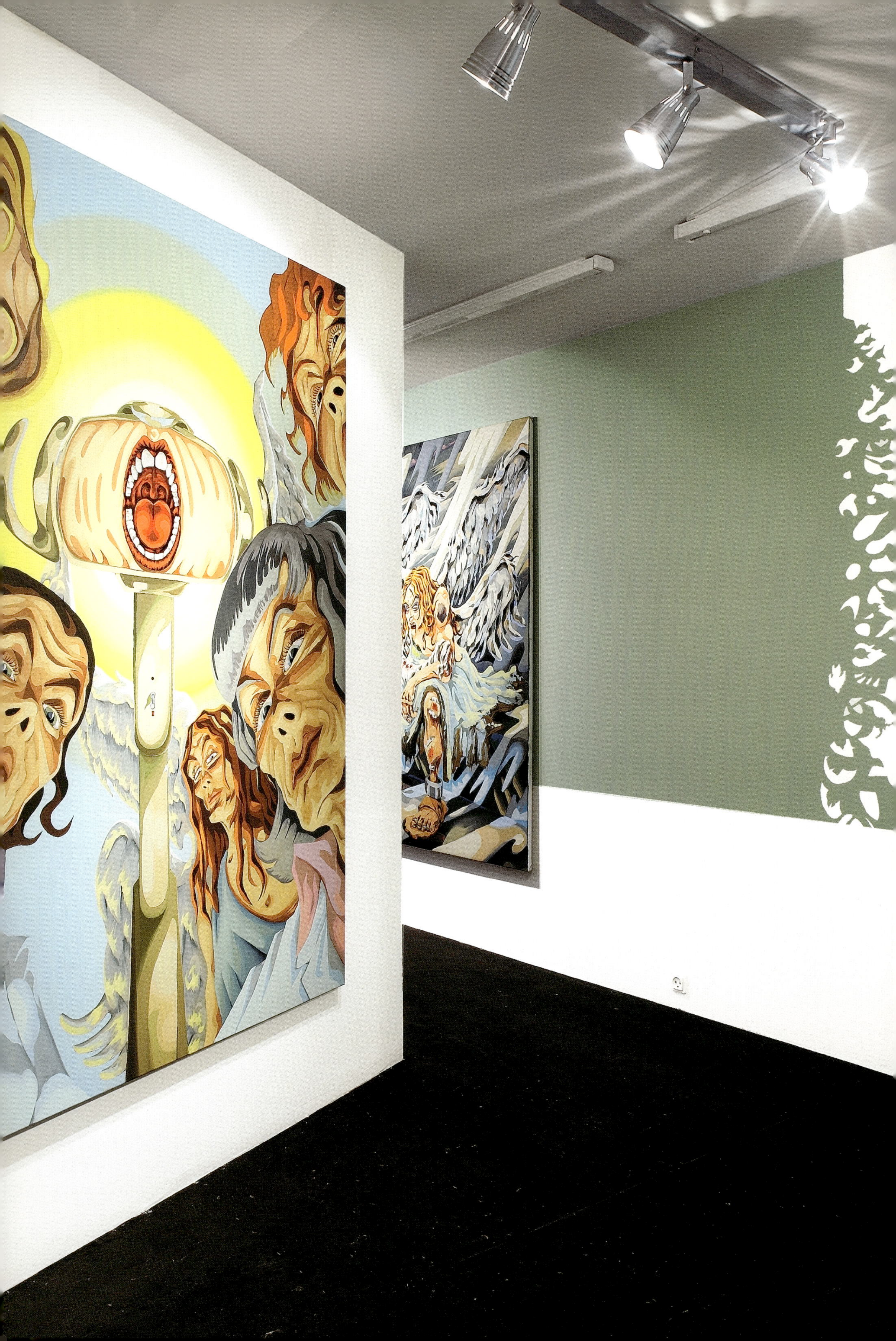

Merete Sanderhoff

Realities

An old myth says that the art of imitating reality came into being in Antiquity, as a young woman drew an outline of her lover's shadow cast on a wall. This little story institutes the concept that art can be a direct, 1:1 representation of visible reality. Ever since, the relationship between art and reality has been a subject of discussion and examination. This has resulted in both praise of and skepticism toward art able to seduce the eye into believing in the illusion of representation.

For the last hundred years this skepticism has been pronounced. Modern consciousness implies recognizing that figurative representation, however truthful or apt it might seem, is always constituted by a system of signs *designating* something without *being* it. Reality cannot be reached through a picture—there will always be a displacement from the real to the picture plane when art is imitating its subject.

You might ask, however, what is *real*? There is the objective reality, which everyone can agree on. But is God real? For a believer, yes, but for a non-believer God is an idea. Are ideas real? Are dreams? Is a reality show on TV? "Everything in this world is a proposal of reality," says Martin Bigum. When he makes art he does it from what he sees. "It might be phantoms, illusions, and visions. That doesn't make them less real." It is obvious to anyone who sees his paintings that they are not outlines of shadows in 1:1, as in the ancient myth, but rather the results of an artist's personal experience and versioning of reality. When Bigum speaks of reality here, he includes subjective sensation and reflection. This does not necessarily mean, however, that this concept of reality is delimited to a singular individual—it can easily be collective. 1.7 billion Christians can't be wrong. Even if the issue is actually subjective interpretations of reality, together they might seem objectively real.

References

In his series of artworks *The Face of God*, 2002–2006, Bigum explores subjective realities that are simultaneously collective and therefore might look like objective facts. In pictures of gods and angels, mythological figures from high as well as popular culture, and culturally defined authorities such as priests, doctors, judges, and parents, he investigates the notions of reality that determine and control peoples' actions without necessarily being real in the objective sense of the word. These more or less abstract figures share the fact that they are not human conditions unless they are instituted as such, individually or collectively: belief, tradition, convention, ideology, chance, fate, roots.

Like a devil's advocate, Bigum releases these mythologically defined
authorities from their metaphorical space, turning them into concrete,
life-like figures. This enables him to pose the question of their reality very
poignantly, and with that, explore how human patterns of reaction are
constructed. What expectations to ourselves and to existence make us
put confidence in authorities like gods or pop idols? What mechanisms
make us fear change, fate, death, or the verdict of our surroundings?
Questions like these emerge from *The Face of God* and Bigum, being the
kind of artist who wants to involve the spectator in his large-scale
existentialistic reflections, uses humor, intense colors and compositions,
and an imagination growing wild, to consciously seduce us into going
along with the game. That is his way of inviting us to investigate the
secrets of the collective, subjective notions of reality, in order to reach
a level of outlook that we normally only attribute to the authorities we
look up to. Behind the humorous and colorful surface of *The Face of God*
lies a seriously subversive message.

Bigum's use of recognizable figures from widespread mythologies ranging from the sacred to the utmost profane, is part of his scheme to
seduce the spectator into the deeply serious core of his work. The
special attraction of Bigum's paintings is how he uses these ingrained
images, first as eye catchers, and later on to tilt the clichés into new
recognition. The use of quotations and references provides a common
starting point for interpretation and comprehension, opening up the
spectator's own reservoir of cultural luggage. Bigum's knack is to distort
and bewitch our collective memory by letting quotations from fundamen-
tally different spheres collide in the same picture. As in *Sacred and
Profane*, 2003, where a centuries-old picture of Hell in the tradition of
Hieronymus Bosch meets satirist Wallace Wood's vision of what you might
call "Disneyland After Dark." Or as in *Red Right Hand*, 2003, where an
army of grinning Robin Hood's offer their charity with blood red right
hands, quoting Nick Cave's song about the Evil One. Or as in *Vanity Fair*,
2005, where the literary couples Sherlock Holmes & Dr Watson, Don
Quixote & Sancho Panchas, Robinson Crusoe & Friday are summoned with
God & Jesus and the Priest & the Devil. All conventional ideas about
these mythological figures are turned upside down, and the spectator is
invited to ponder and form his/her own hierarchies. The title *Vanity Fair*,
moreover, is exemplary in simultaneously referring to Thackeray's literary
classic and the American lifestyle magazine of the same name.

Correspondences

Once you are tempted to enter Bigum's universe in search of more quotes
and puns to ponder, and you immerse yourself in the question of human
notions of reality, *The Face of God* begins to disperse into sub-series of
pictures corresponding particularly with each other. One of these sub-
series might be the long row of paintings composed as accumulations of
similar figures filling up the canvas right to the edge of the frame (e.g.
Terrified Surgeons, 2003; *Bitter Judges*, 2004; *Disappointed Gods*, 2002;
Priests, 2004; *Disappointed Mothers*, 2003). In several of these pictures
you notice how the individual figures gathered within the frame are de-
prived of their individuality and melt together in telling ways. The gods'

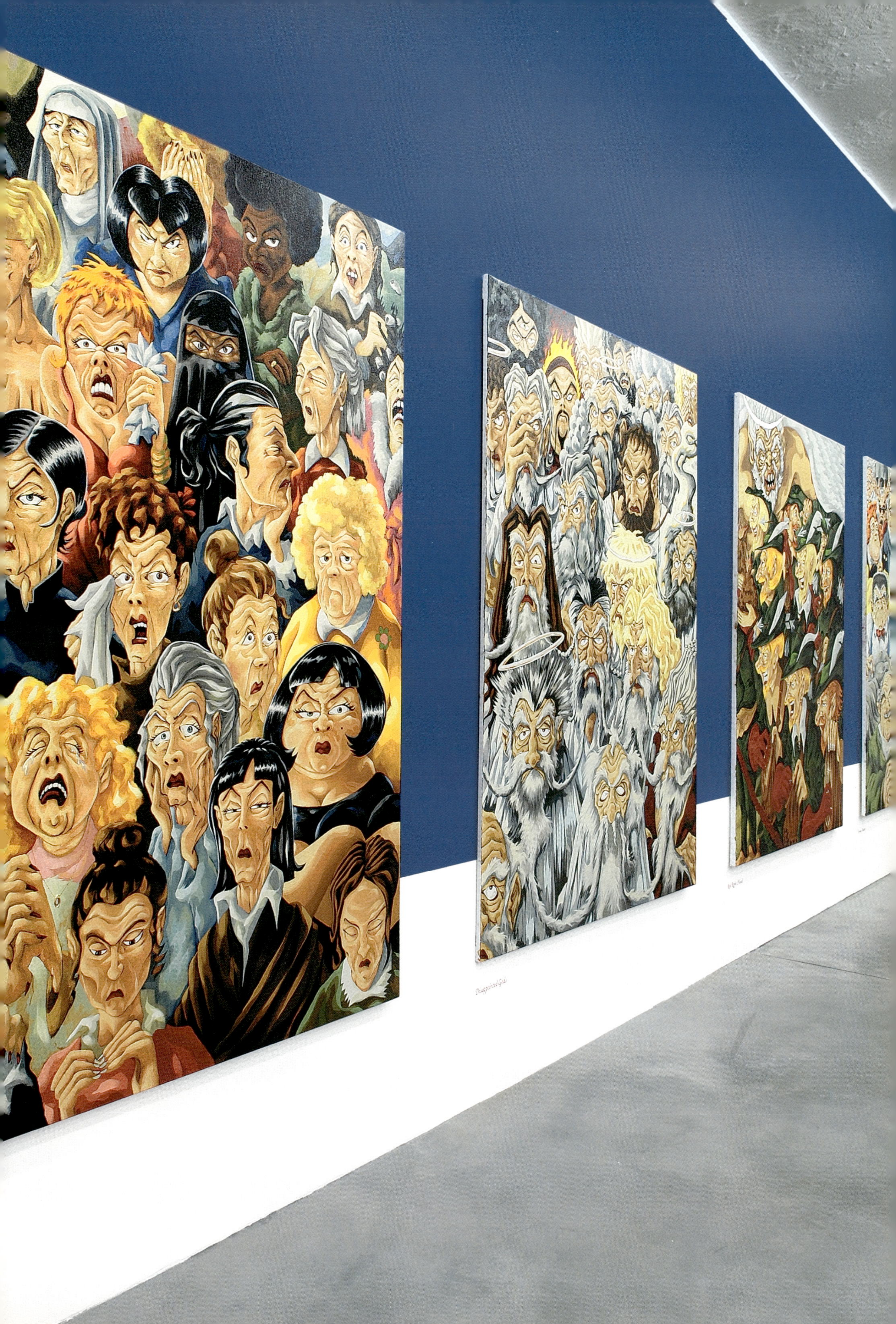

Disappointed Gods

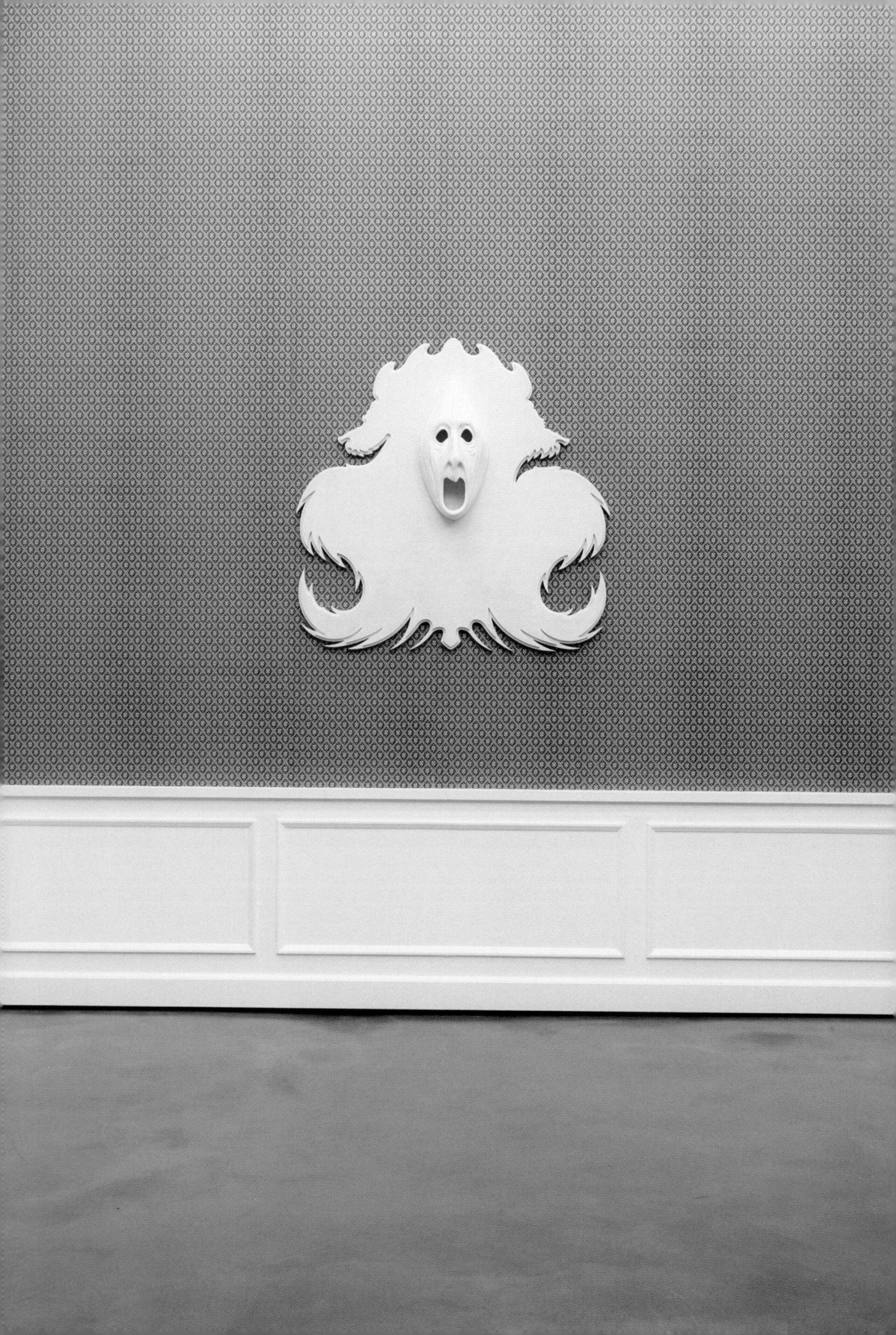

long beards weave into each other, making the different religions they represent appear confusingly similar. Recognizing how images of gods are generally of a piece, an obvious reaction would be to marvel at the bloody battles people all over the world engage in, in defense of their particular religion. *Priests* hint in the same direction, as the Christian priest in the foreground is suddenly Hinduized, as the figure immediately above him lending him his blue cloak as a turban.

Another sub-series explores the artistic relation to and interpretation of reality (e.g. *The Mouth of Hell*, 2005; *Hymn (S.U. Thomsen)*, 2002–2003; *Vision and Fact*, 2004–2005). These works all contain crevices in representation, forming entrances to other worlds. In *Hymn* the space behind the Danish poet Søren Ulrik Thomsen is torn like a curtain, revealing a metaphysical ocean of burning candles (referring to his poem *Mit lys brænder*, "my candle is burning"). *Vision and Fact* presents a different kind of torn curtain. Eight pictures, that seem to be sketches and ideas for other paintings in *The Face of God*, are placed around a white silhouette of a wanderer, forming a visual opening in the wall that reminds you of the holes Tom & Jerry make when they crash through a fence or penetrate the surface of the earth at great speed. Bigum uses the same image of the wanderer, who has left this world for another, in different places in his oeuvre, e.g. in his poem *Poet-etik*, 2006, where he is shown passing through the mouth of Hell.

"The Mouth of Hell is in the Face of God." These are Bigum's own words. And the dilemma of art, you might add, if you tackle it the way Bigum does. The attempt to approach an absolute, "divine" outlook and insight (what Bigum calls the *Face of God*) inevitably leads to a point where the artistic vision must be translated in order to be transmitted. A painter translates his vision into shadows on a wall. How are they supposed to catch and contain the complexity of everything imagined? This question has been the struggle of artists through all times and surfaces again in a different shape in *The Great Divide*, 2006, where hordes of men astride fragile soap bubbles are tearing along in a vain quest for the perfect expression. The soap bubble is one of the most subtle vanity symbols within 17th-century still-life painting. Bigum's quotation of it becomes a metaphor of the artist's *Dance of Death* with reality.

Bigum is a classically work-oriented painter who works through each painting, enabling it to stand on its own two feet and communicate an integrated narrative. At the same time he passes through larger themes in series of works which thematically and formally correspond, and in their interplay expand and vary the story of the individual work. *The Face of God*'s basic theme, concerning the authorities formed by and controlling human conceptions and actions, is thus shown in many facets and temperaments during the course of the series. Among the vast group of caricatured figure images, a few pictures stand out, playing on very different poetical and structural gamuts (e.g. *Swift Bird*, 2004; *Hospital View*, 2006). Noticing, however, the compositional and conceptual links between, for example, *Swift Bird* and *Limbo*, 2005, leading on to *Terrified Surgeons*, and *Hospital View*, a melancholic dimension is added to the otherwise rather euphorical pitch of the series.

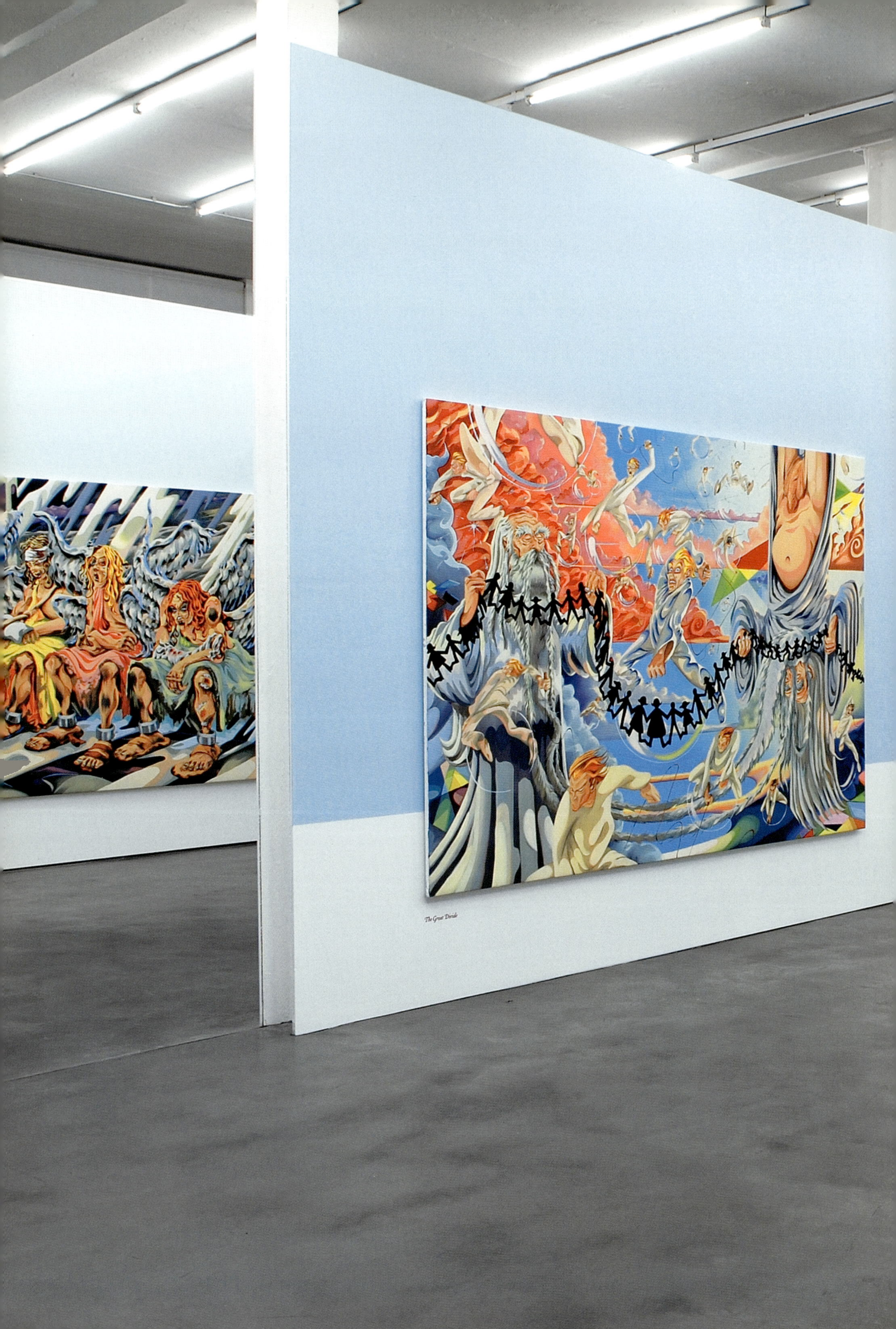

The Great Divide

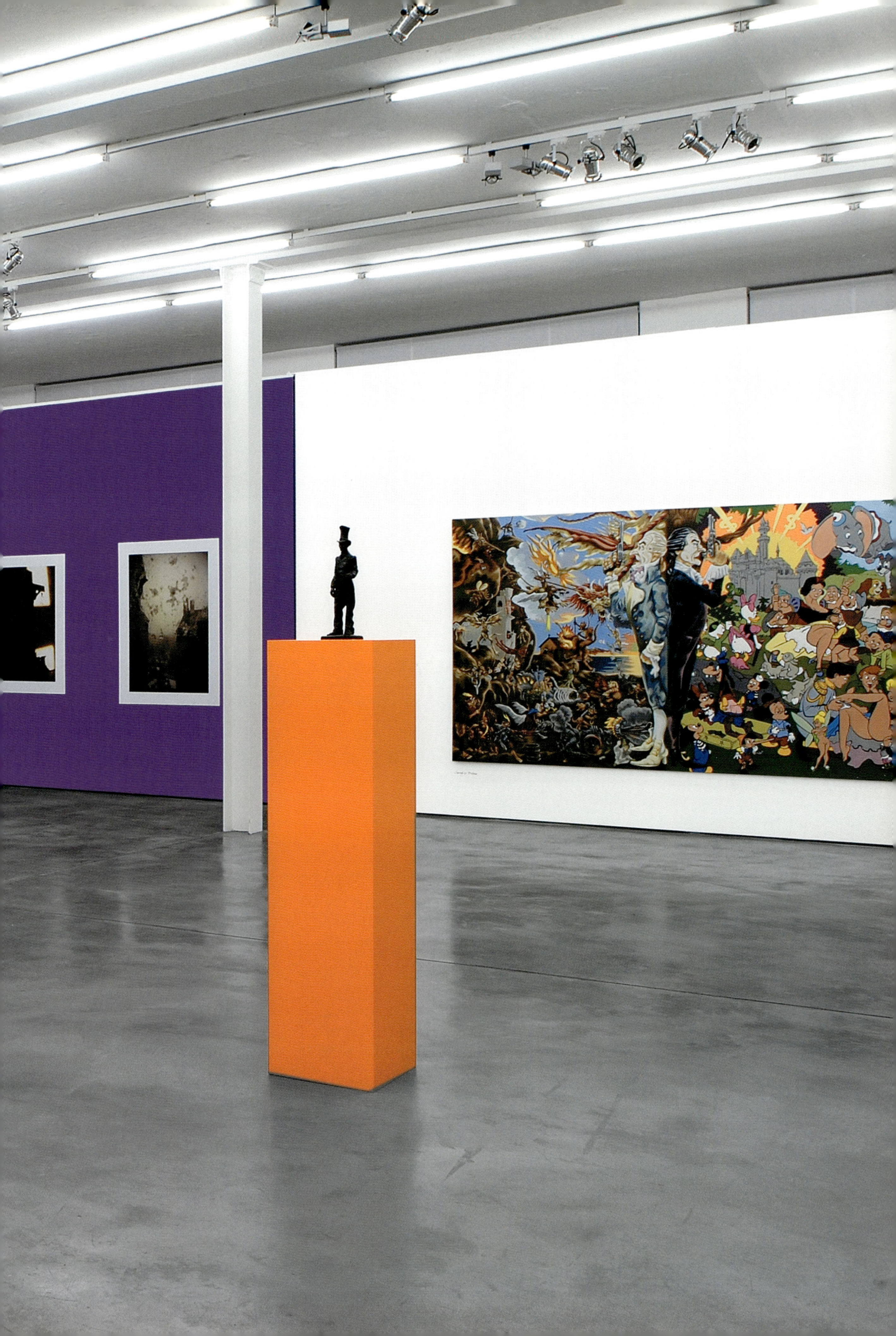

Just as the figures within individual pictures are entangled in each other, all the works in the series are bound together in festoons of premise and consequence. These crisscross correspondences endow the humor and buffoonery with an abrupt sense of gravity, hitting you like splinters of glass from a bewitched mirror. Only then does the dilemma of the series really unfold. It is one thing to dissect and criticize subjective notions of reality that are practised collectively, it is another to put something better, truer, more substantial in its place. Here Bigum is apt to step aside for a while, leaving a space untouched for the spectator to form her own conceptions, like the blank space in *Hospital View*.

<u>Modernities</u>

What do you place in the blank space? The question is whether it is possible at all to maintain the idea of an objective, absolute authority that cannot be relativized, discussed, or called into question. With the death of the great narratives—this common, postmodern idea that all ideologies and authorities have come to an end—we find ourselves in a situation where nothing is sacred anymore, or at least no one agrees on what is sacred. You are free to institute and replace your authorities as you please. The human notions of reality have lost their stability and have become fluid and volatile. They have become exposed as conceptions.

According to the French cultural theorist and philosopher Jean Baudrillard, this exerts a crucial influence on the contemporary constitution of reality. When reality is no longer conceived of as true and absolute, it looses authenticity and sovereignty and is instead split into atoms— proposals of reality. In its logical conclusion, Baudrillard sees this produced in a hyperreality like the one encountered in the media, on www, and increasingly within concrete society, where the real is constructed against a backdrop of conceptual or mythological models without connection to objective reality. These proposals of reality are sometimes of such hallucinatory similarity to *the real thing* that is becomes difficult to tell them apart. Those who are entangled in the illusion are unable to realize their own blindness and experience the replacement or copy of reality as real. The crucial difference is that the copy only imitates the surface of the original, however lacking its content.

One of Martin Bigum's own comments on *The Face of God* goes: "My present is grotesque, caricatured, mimically downhearted, and every meaning either void or hysterical." His diagnosis of the present is in line with Baudrillard's, and is manifested in painting after painting as a mischievous self-conscious play with notions and illusions of reality. As an artist, however, he chooses to be visionary, making paintings that can provide resistance to the apathy of these notions. In his own words, he tries "to demask the myths and expose to the world what is sometimes difficult to recognize." Even though Bigum, on the face of it, looks like the prototype of a postmodern artist with his art-historical cross-references and promiscuous mingling of high and low, he rejects the idea that he is part of a postmodern tendency within art. On the contrary his work insists on the continuous existence of the great narratives, not in the shape of dogmatic and suppressive ideologies, but as narratives about human conditions that are basic and timeless and that might function as openings towards dialogue and insight.

Bigum is more of an enlightened Romantic than a postmodernist. He insists that art can affect human reality and make a difference. On the other hand he willingly acknowledges that his work can be seen as an expression of what he calls a *hyper-modernity*, a kind of modernity taken to its logical conclusion with everything that implies, ranging from the breakdown of value systems and relativism to multiplied identities and masquerade. Here Bigum tears the curtain, so to speak, in a genuine quest for the face behind the mask.

What does he find behind the mask? Is it reality? Real reality? According to Bigum himself it is proposals of reality, a phrase that might sum up the substance of art. It is simulations of reality which, through their sublimated interpretations of the concrete world, open up the possibility of impressing and changing existence.

<u>Literature</u>

Jean Baudrillard, *Simulacra and Simulation*, Ann Arbor 1994.
Martin Bigum, "The Secret of Reality. Notes for *The Face of God*," 2006, printed in this volume, p. 43–47.
Barry Schwabsky, "Questions for Martin Bigum," *The Adventures of Art*, Kunsthallen Brandts Klædefabrik, Odense 1997.

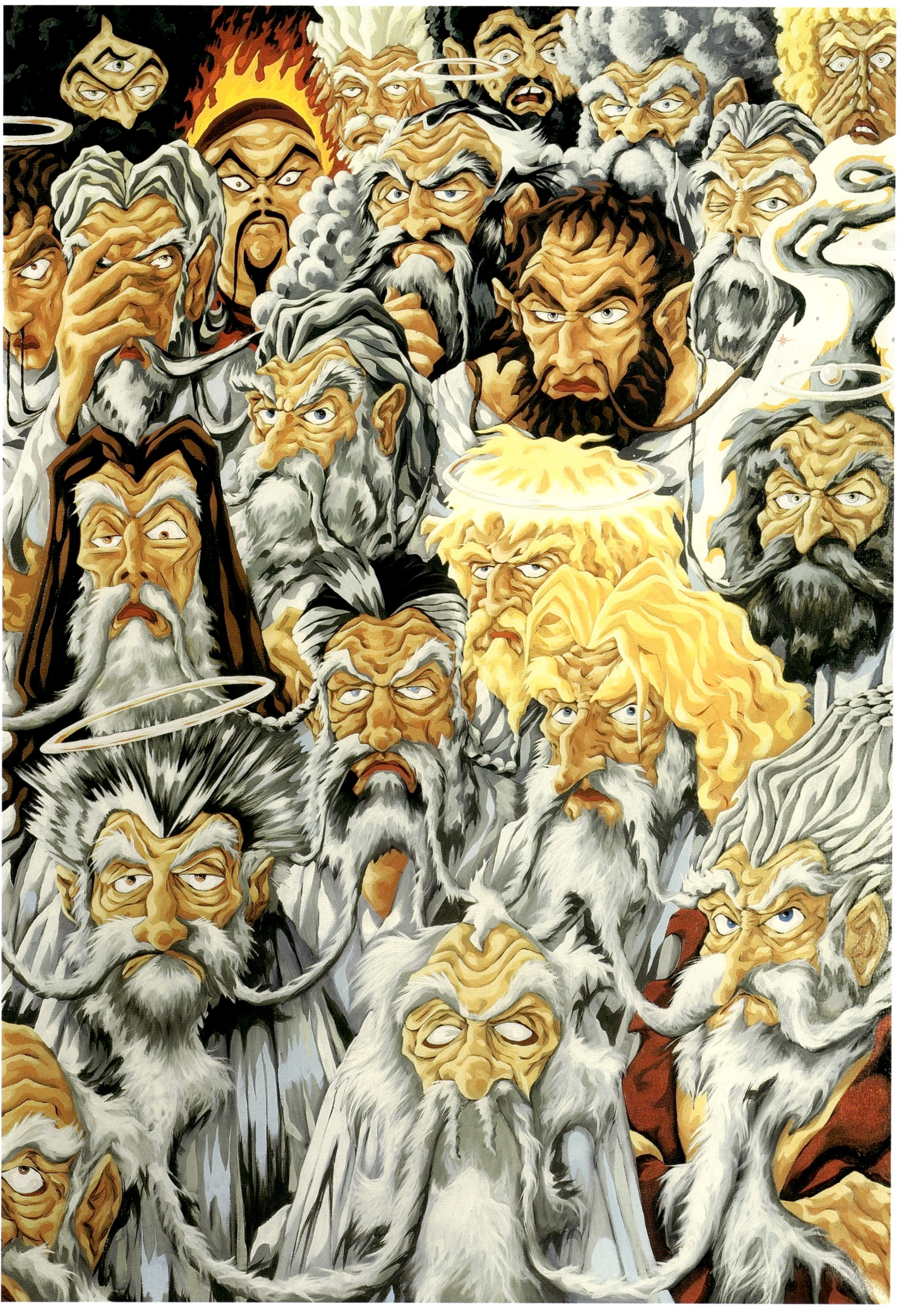

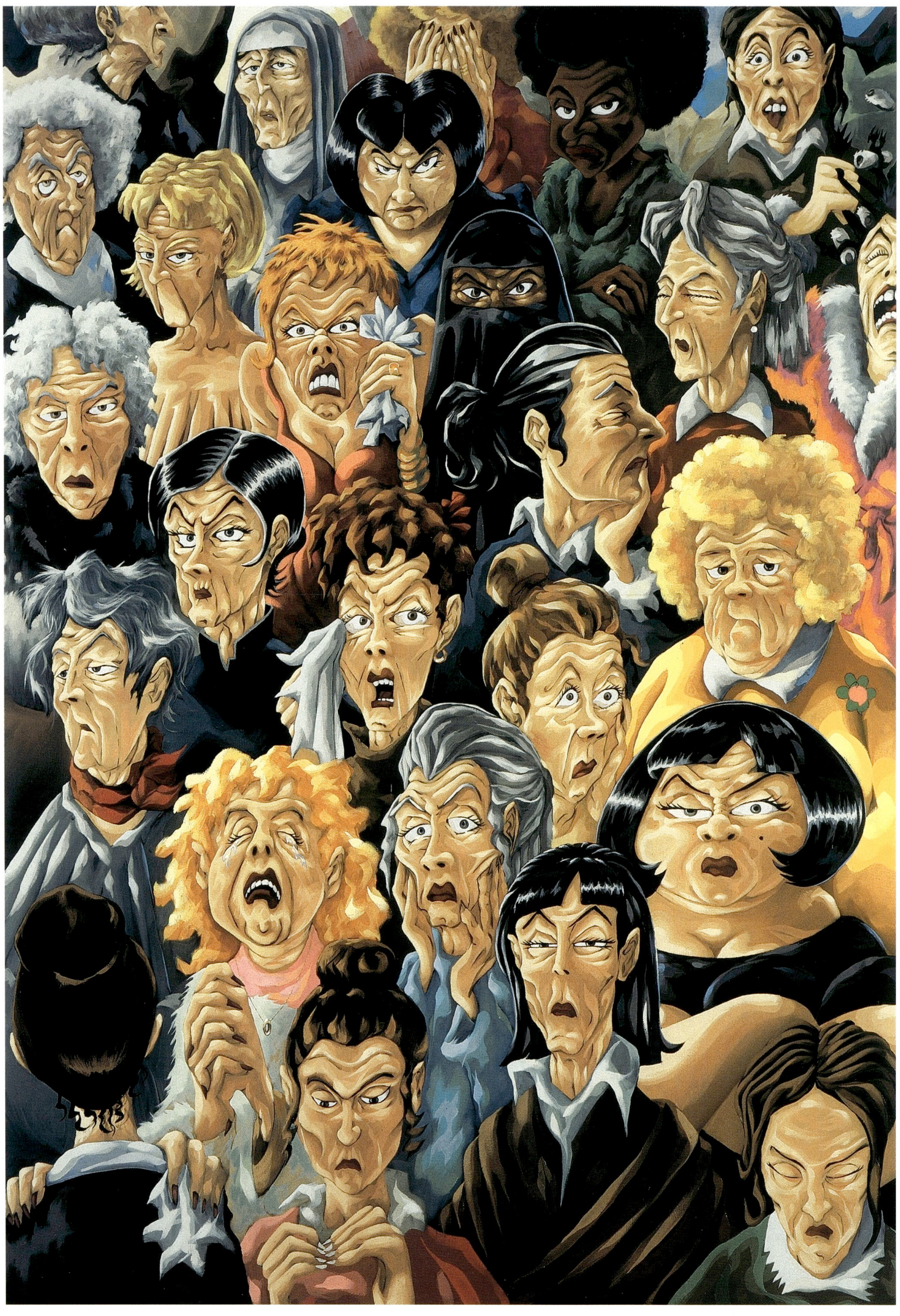

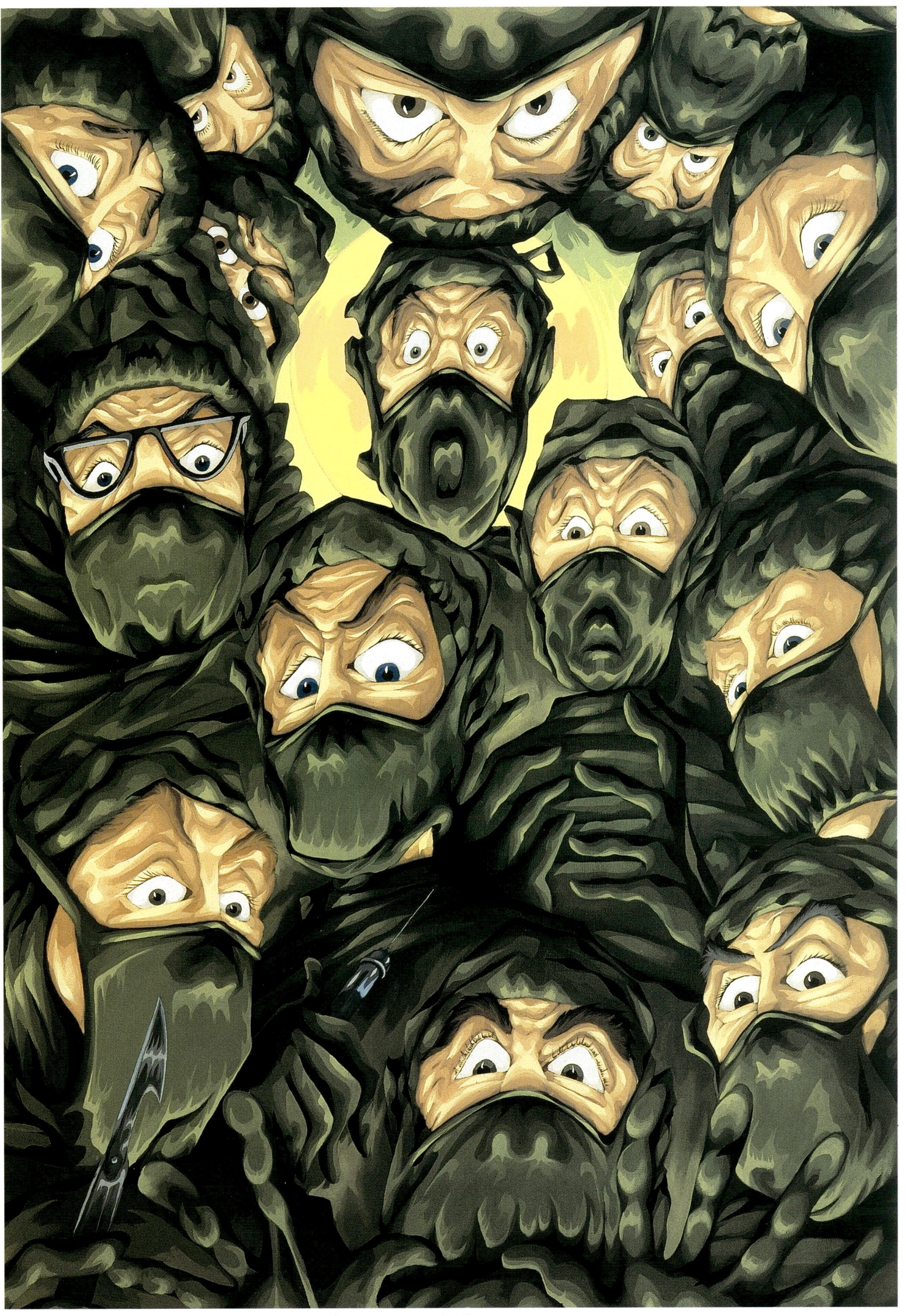

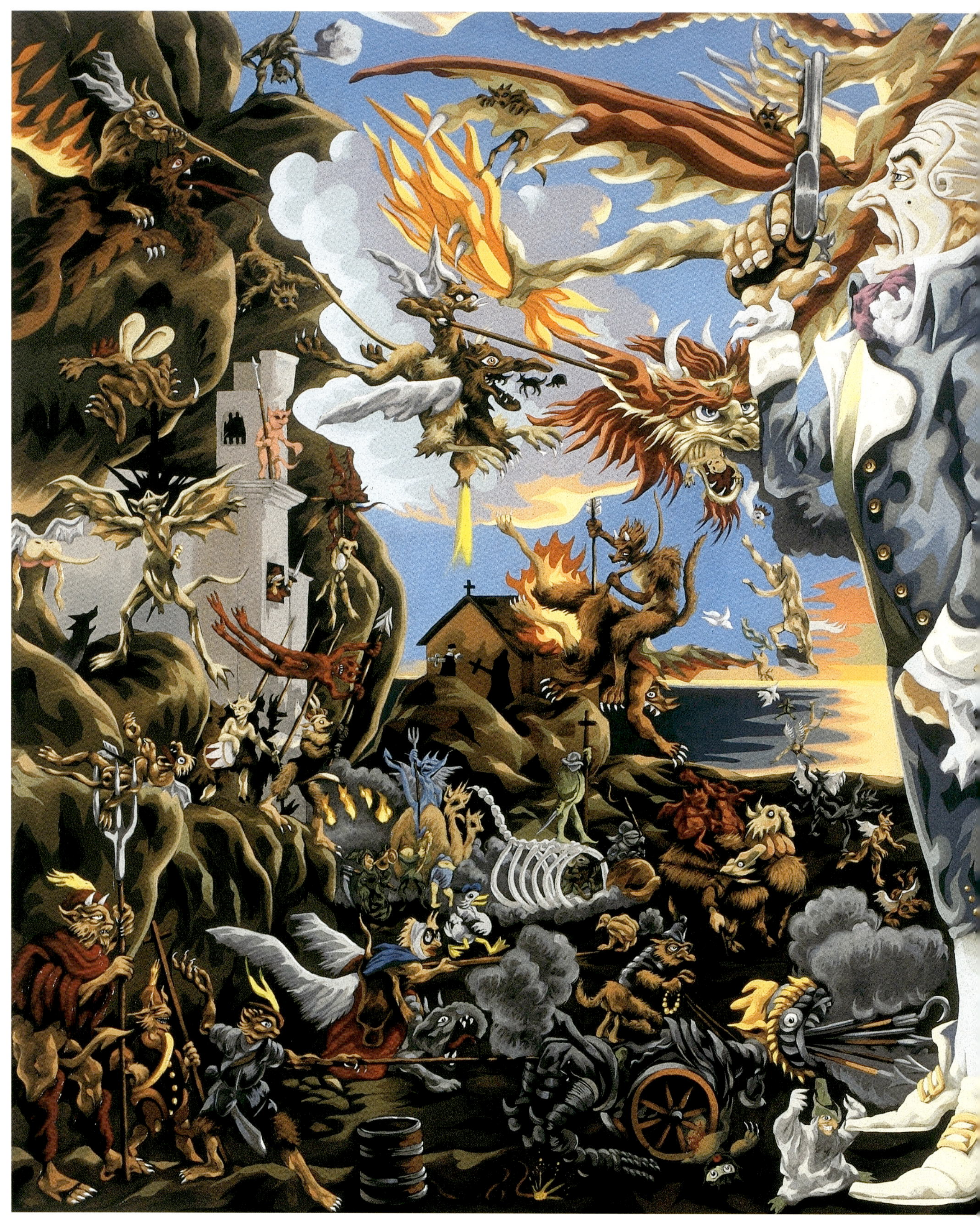

DISAPPOINTED MOTHERS, 2003
← ←

TERRIFIED SURGEONS, 2003
←

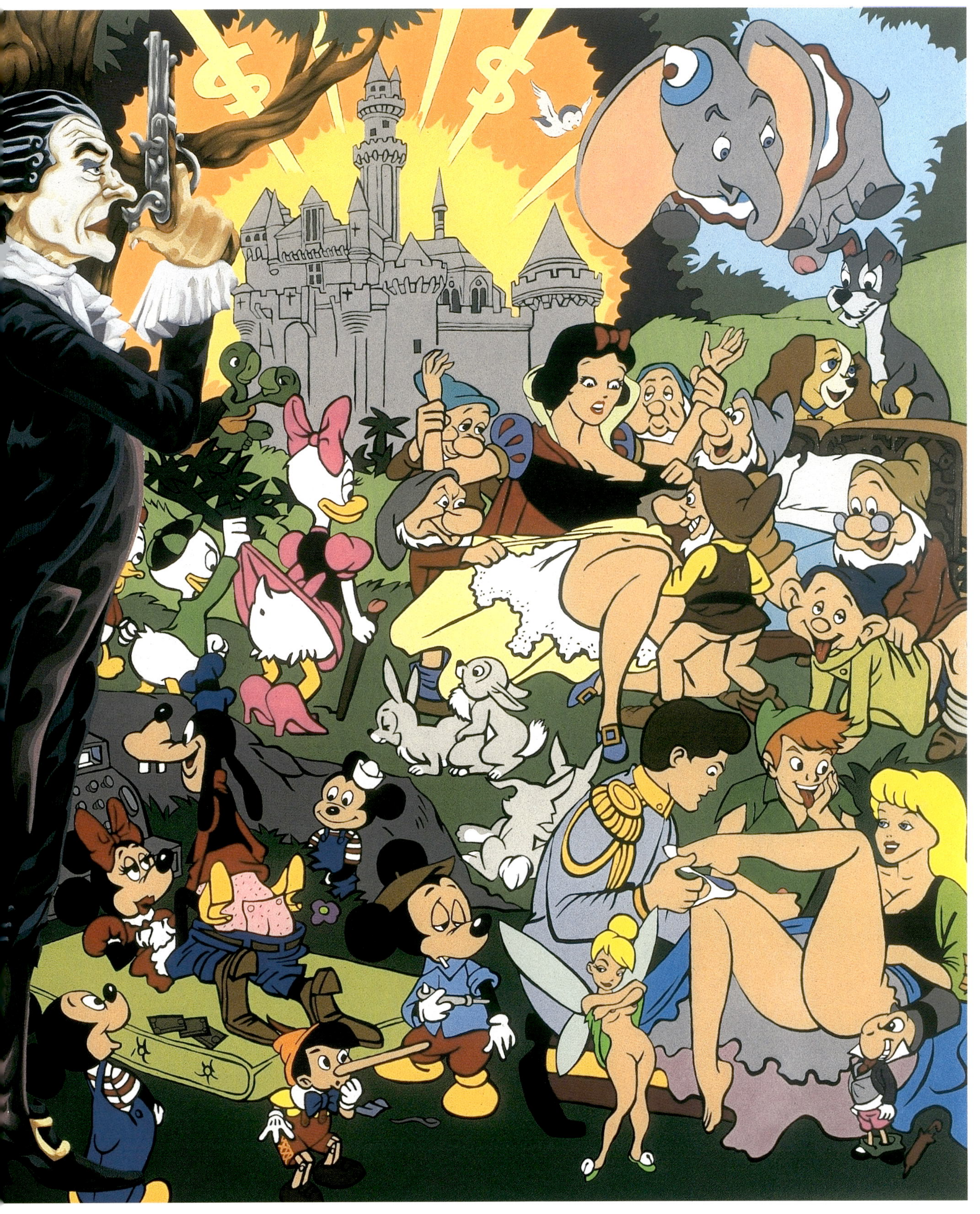

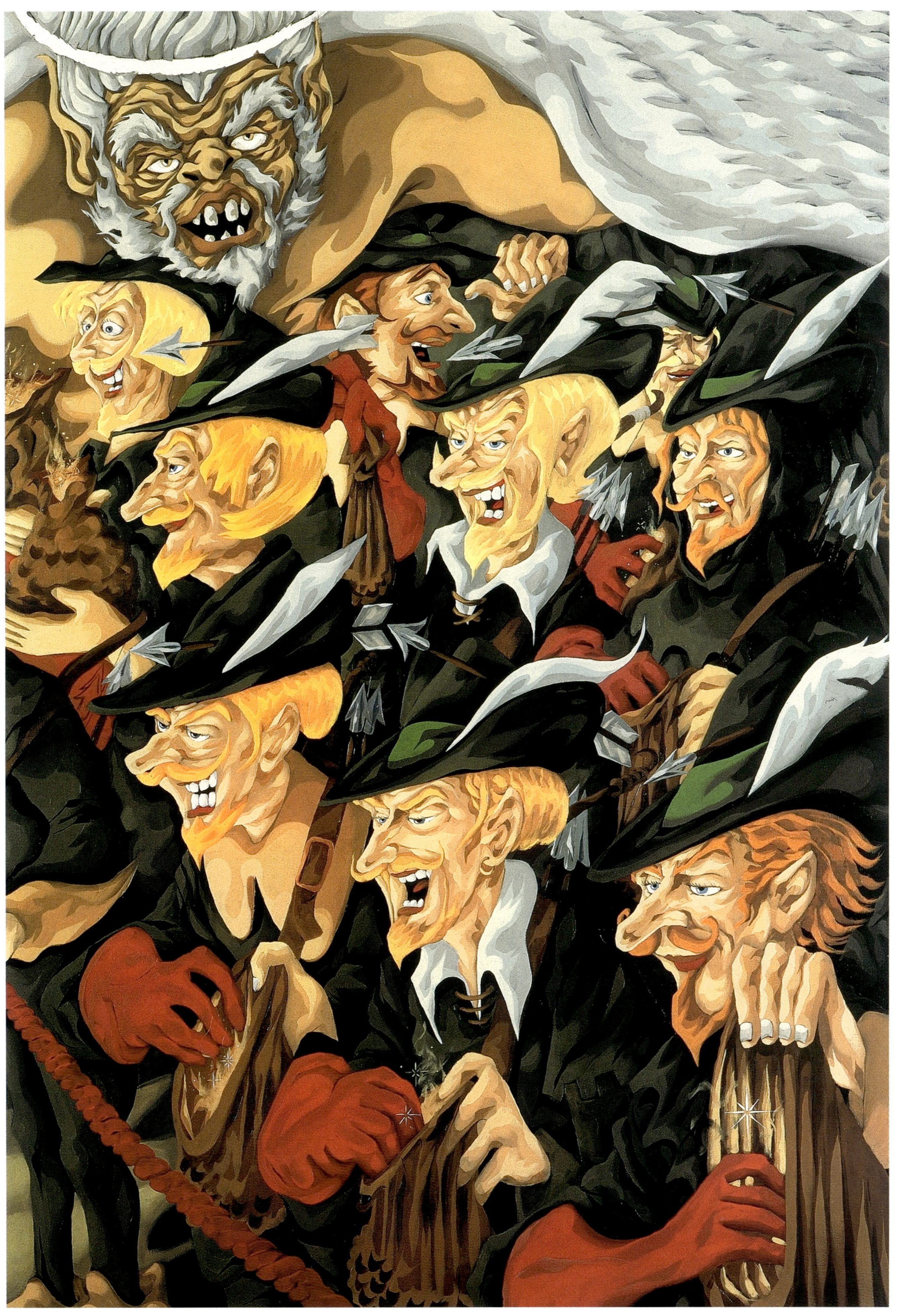

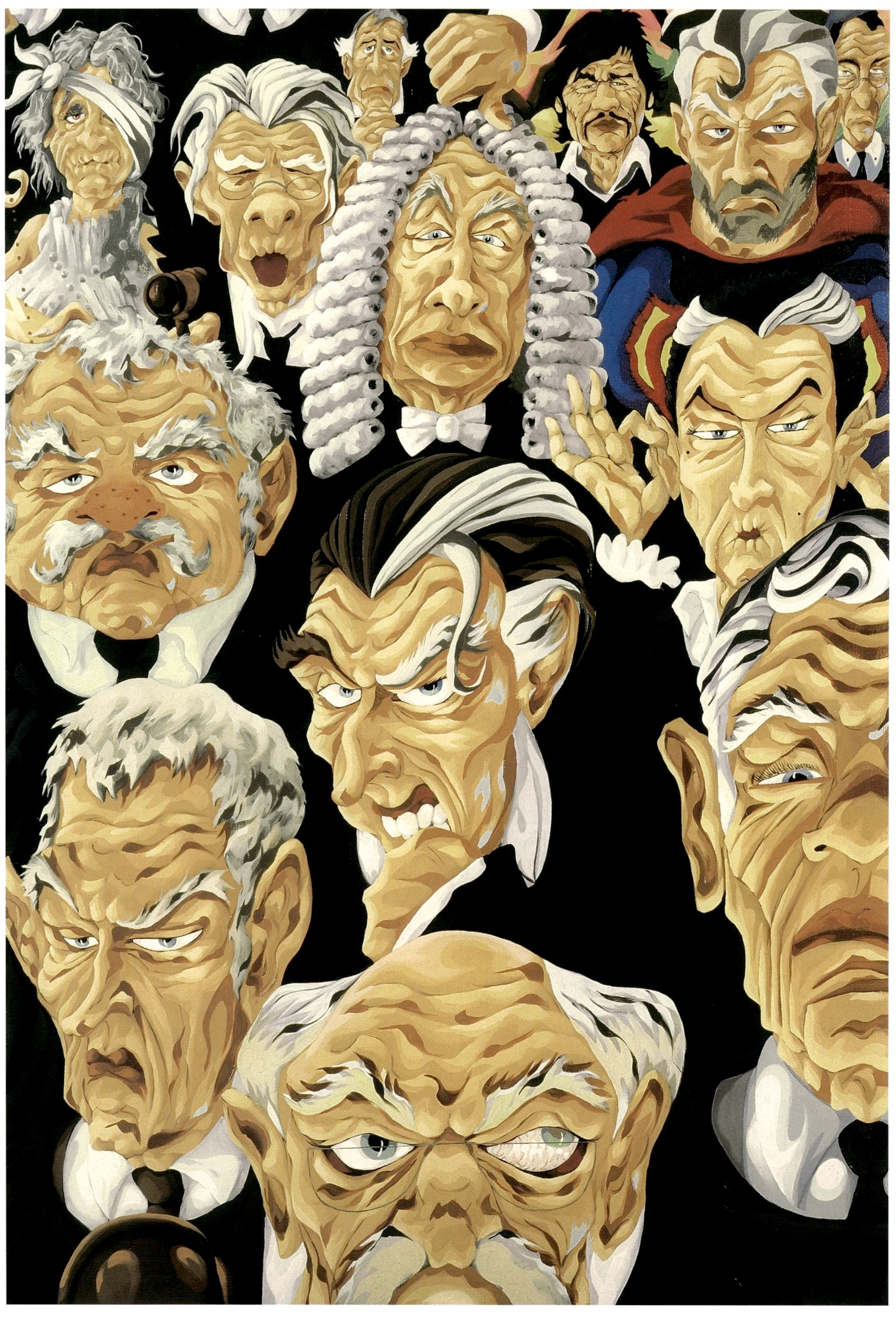

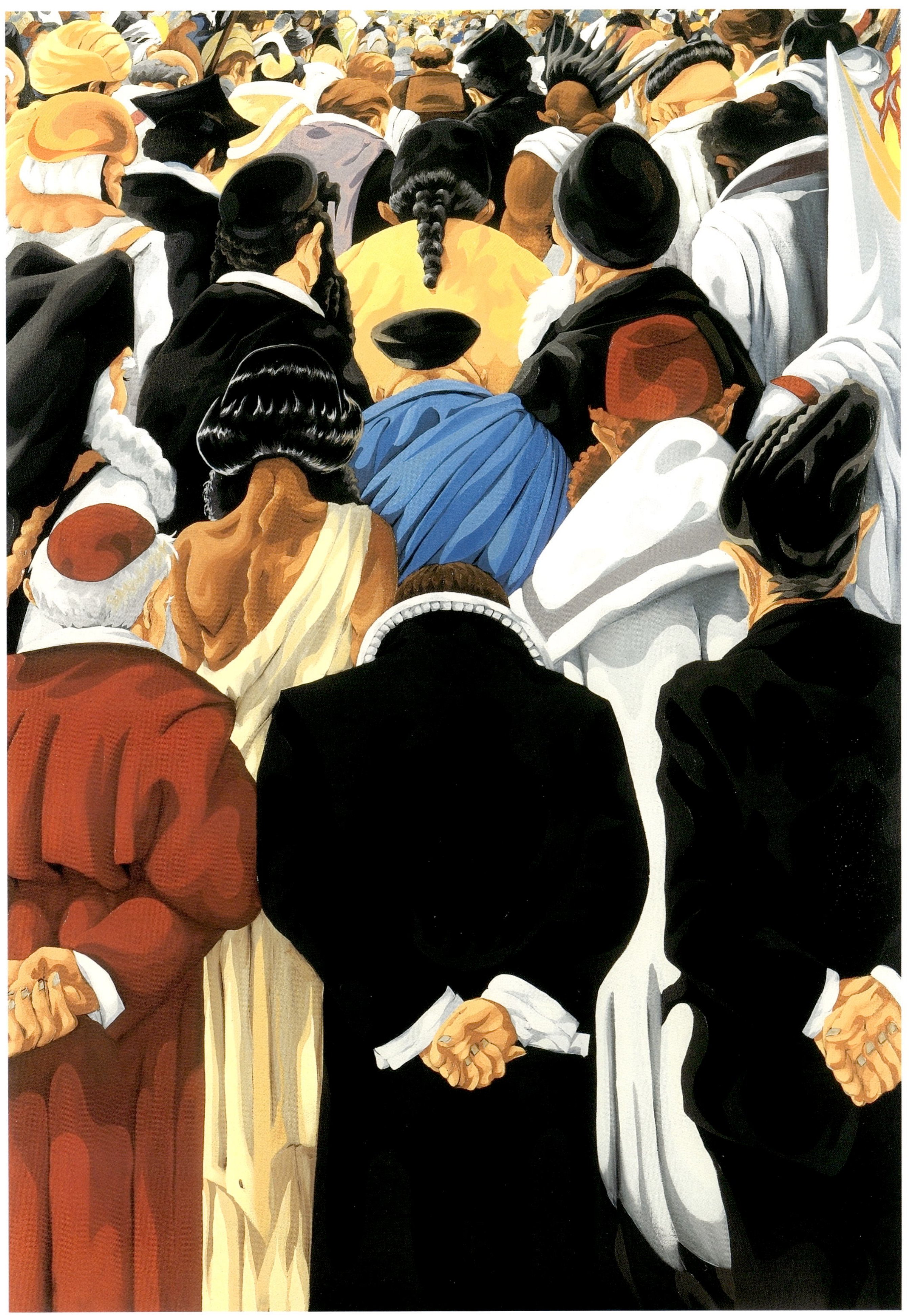

BITTER JUDGES, 2004
← ←

PRIESTS, 2004
←

SWIFT BIRD, 2004
→

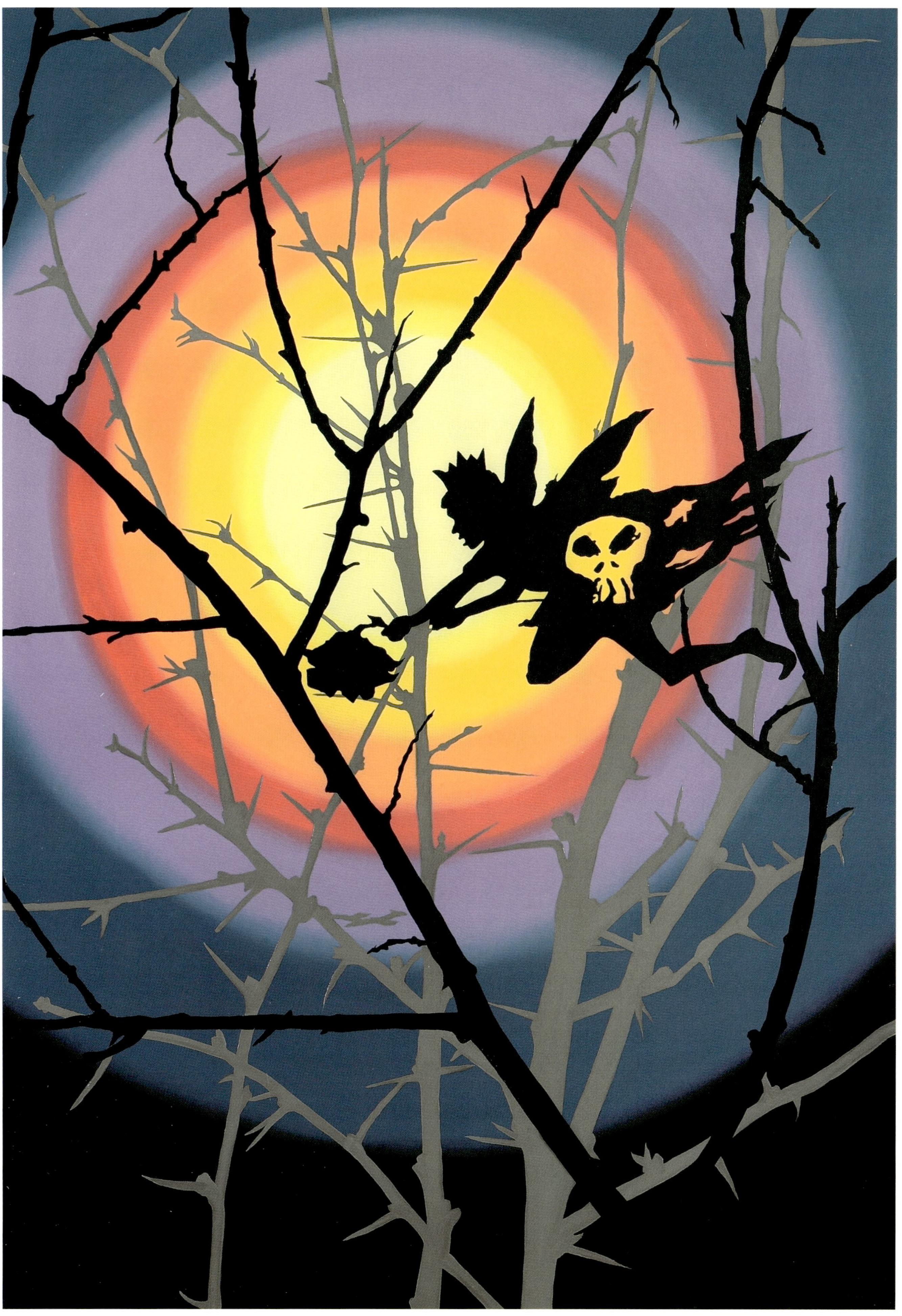

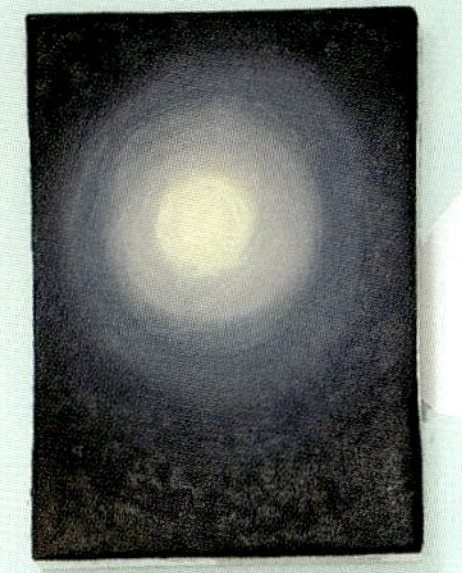
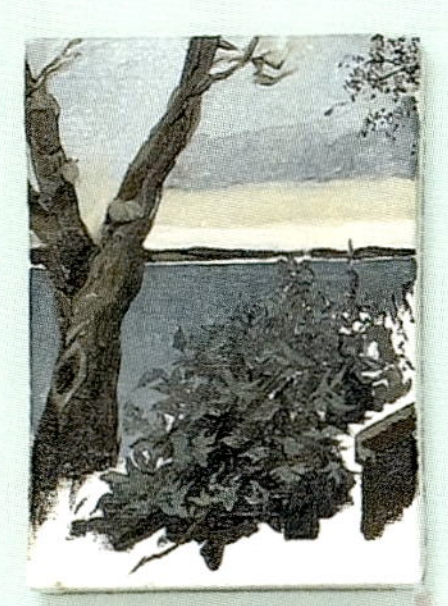
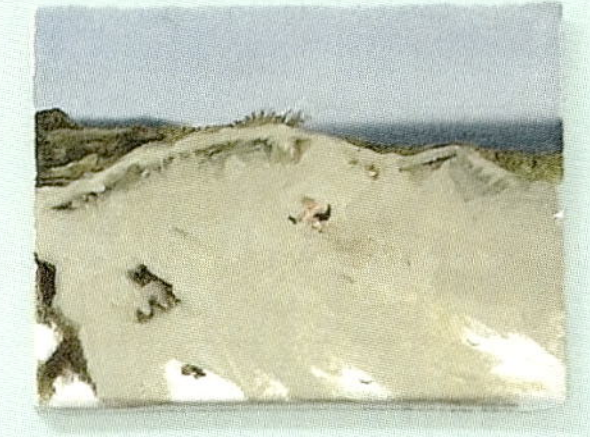
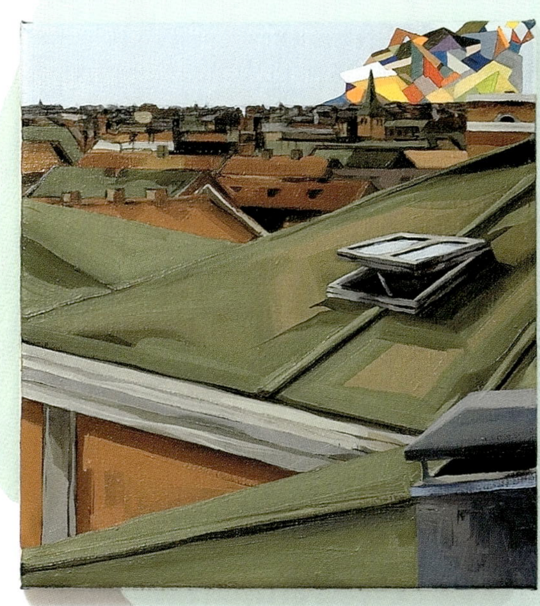
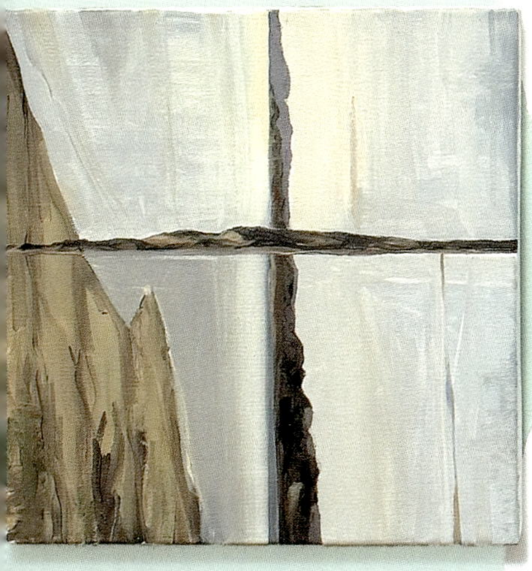
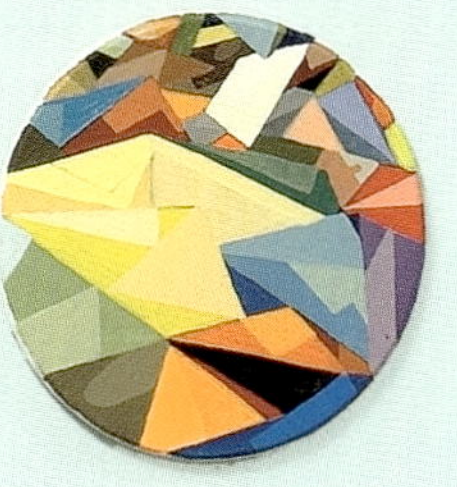
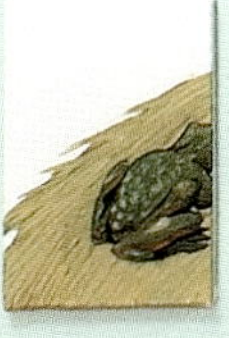
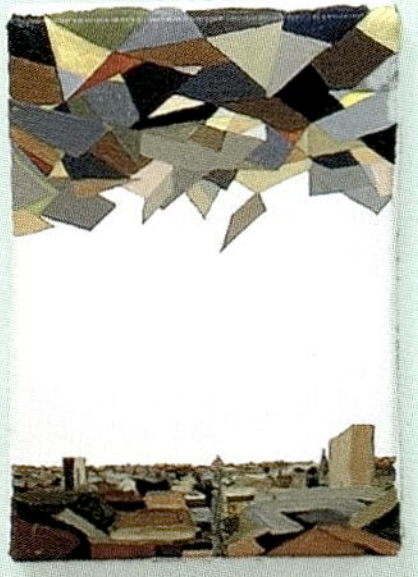

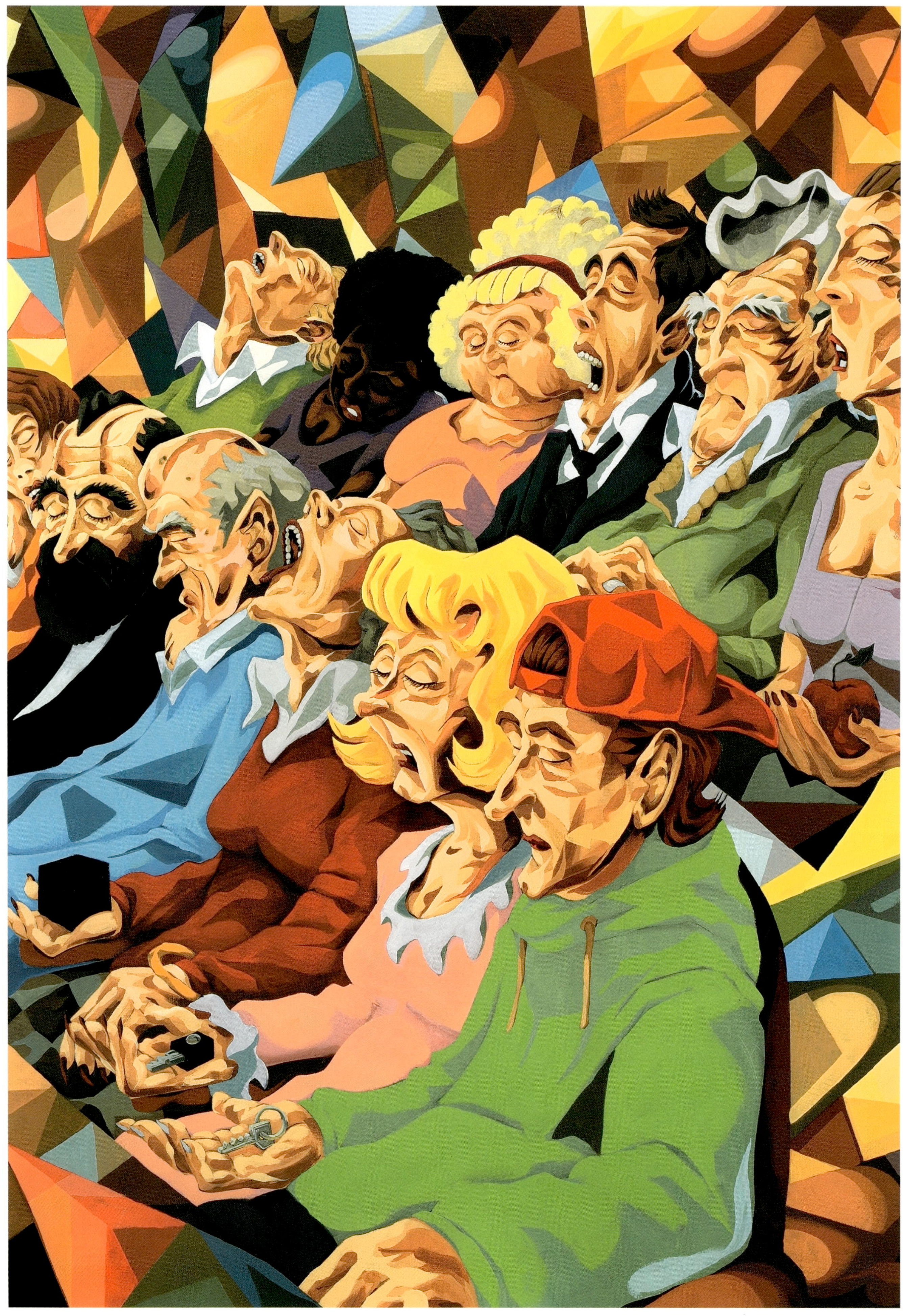

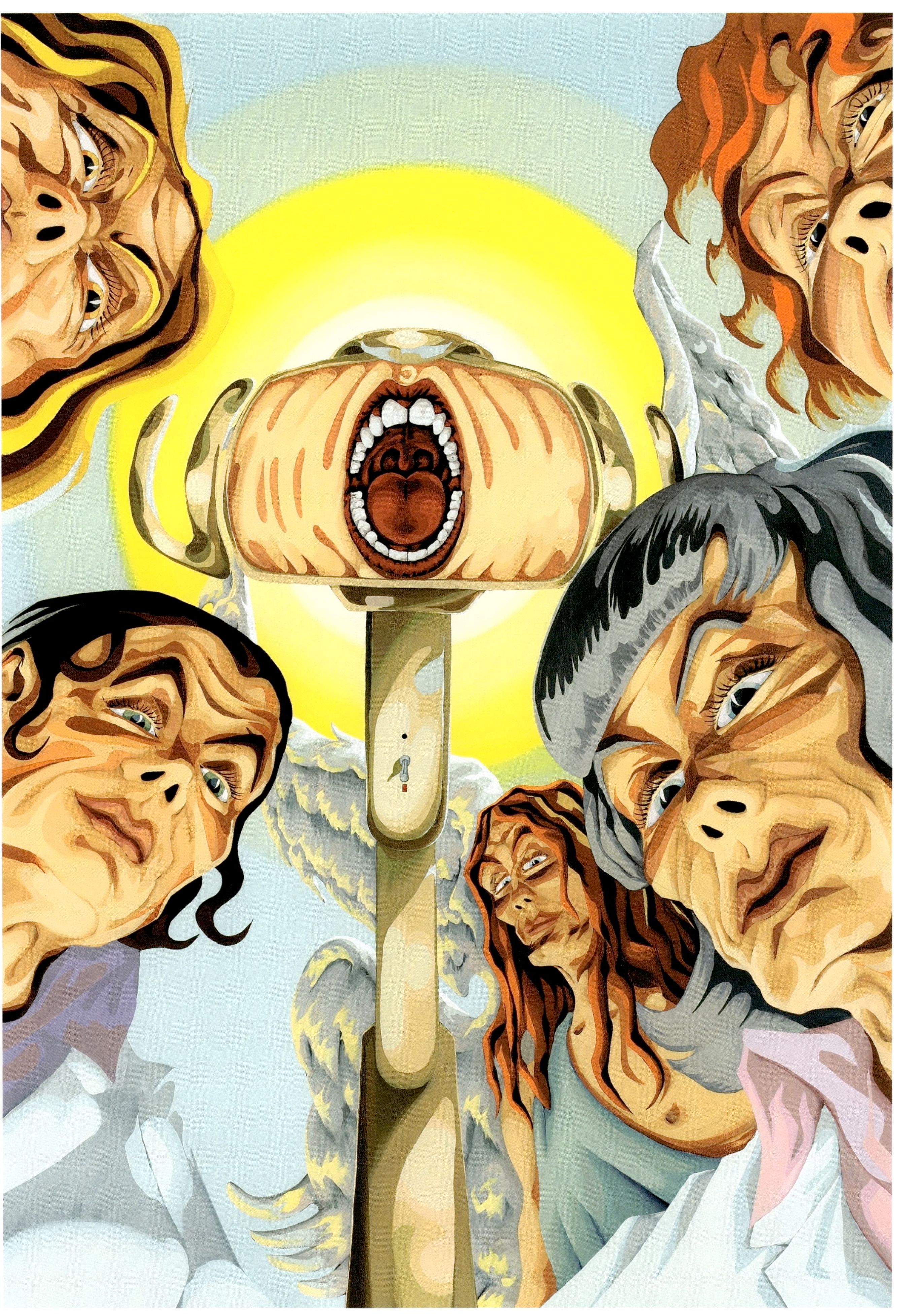

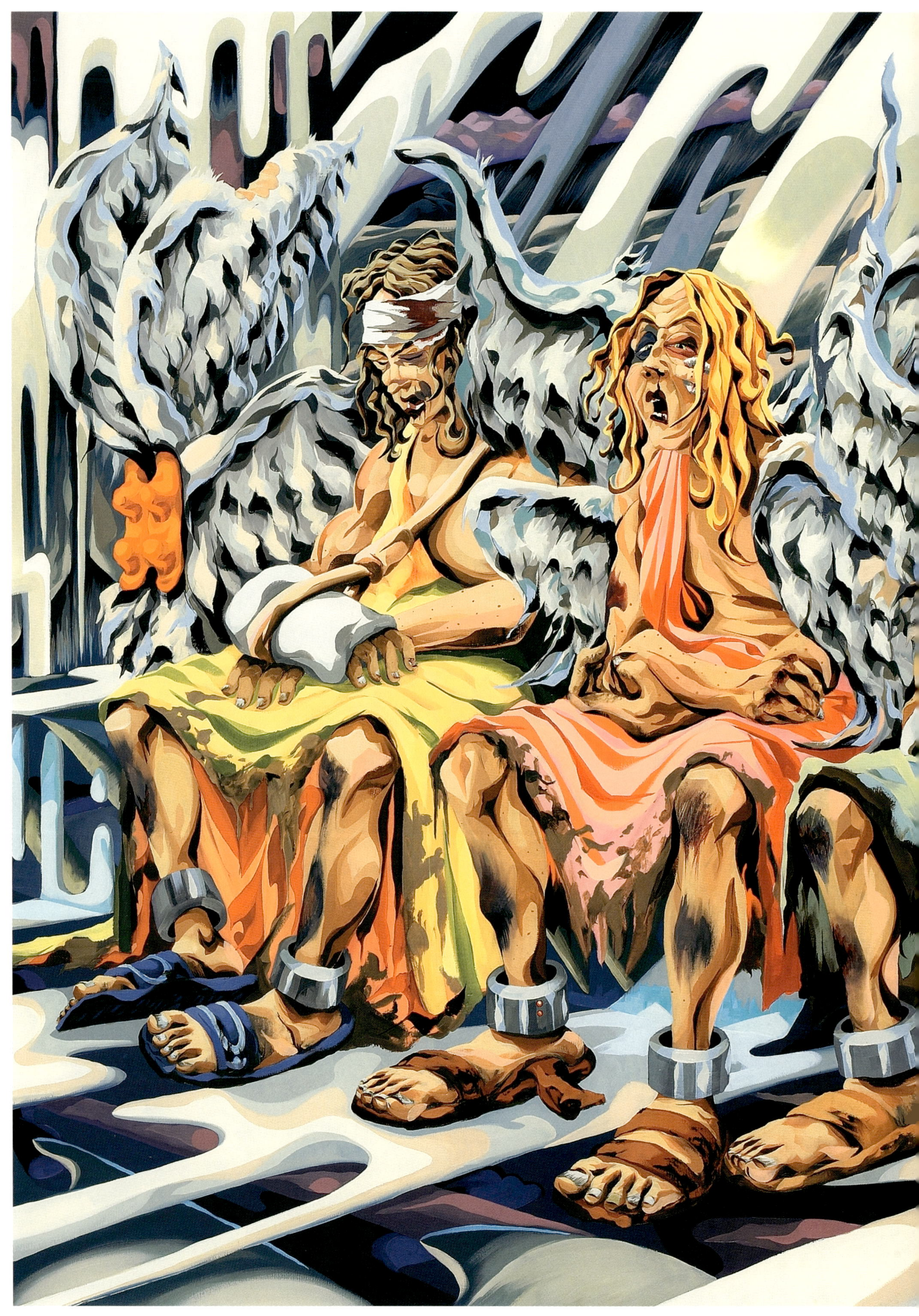

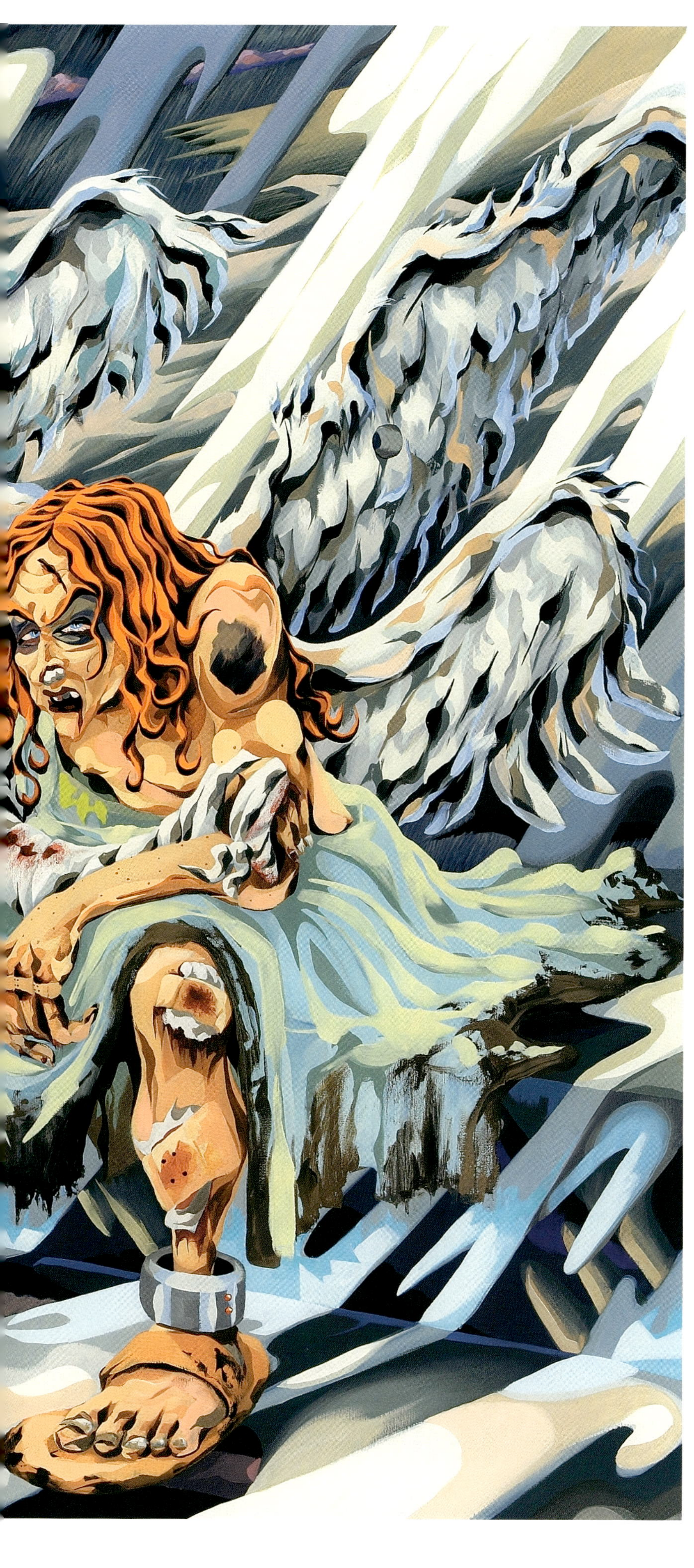

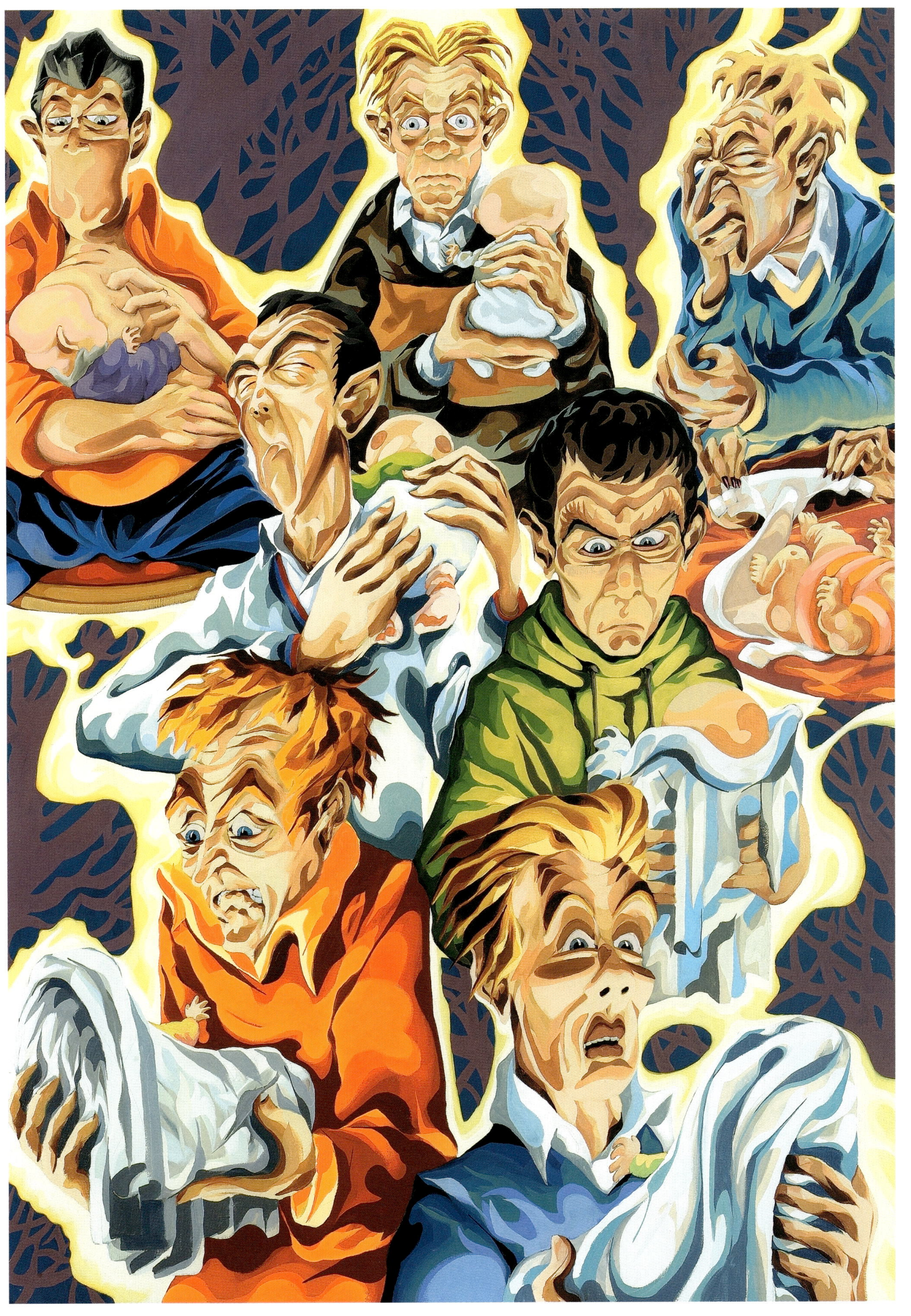

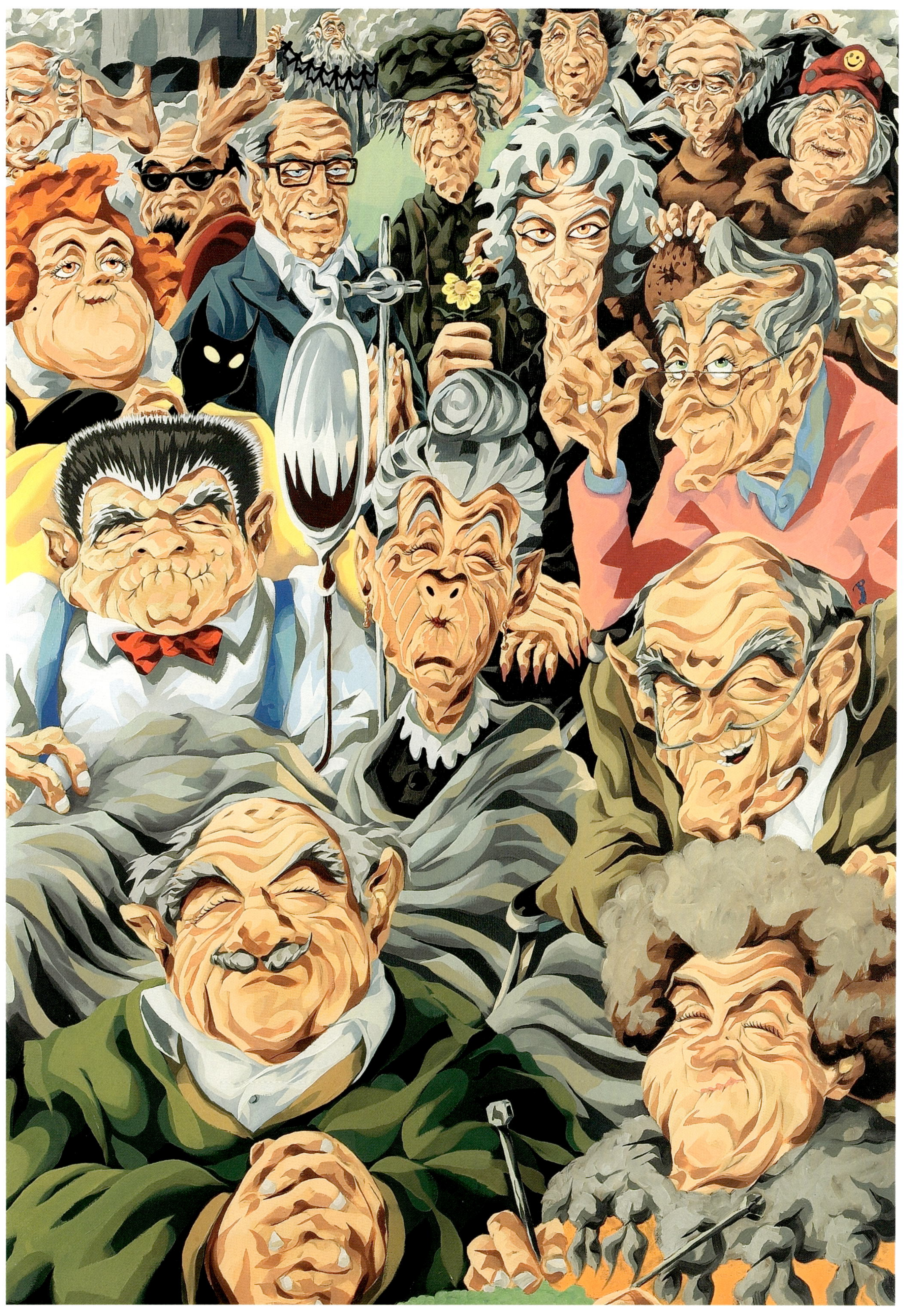

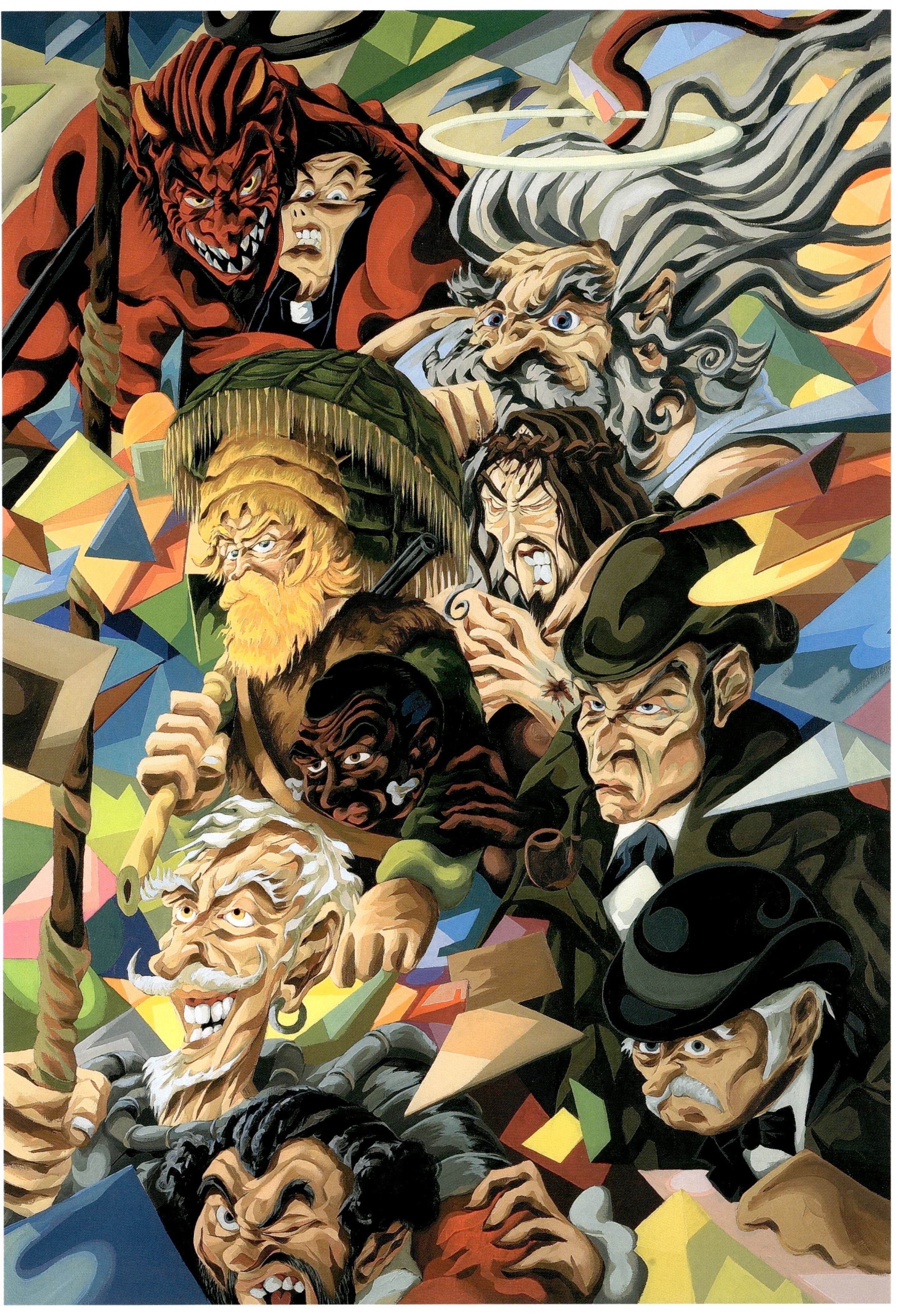

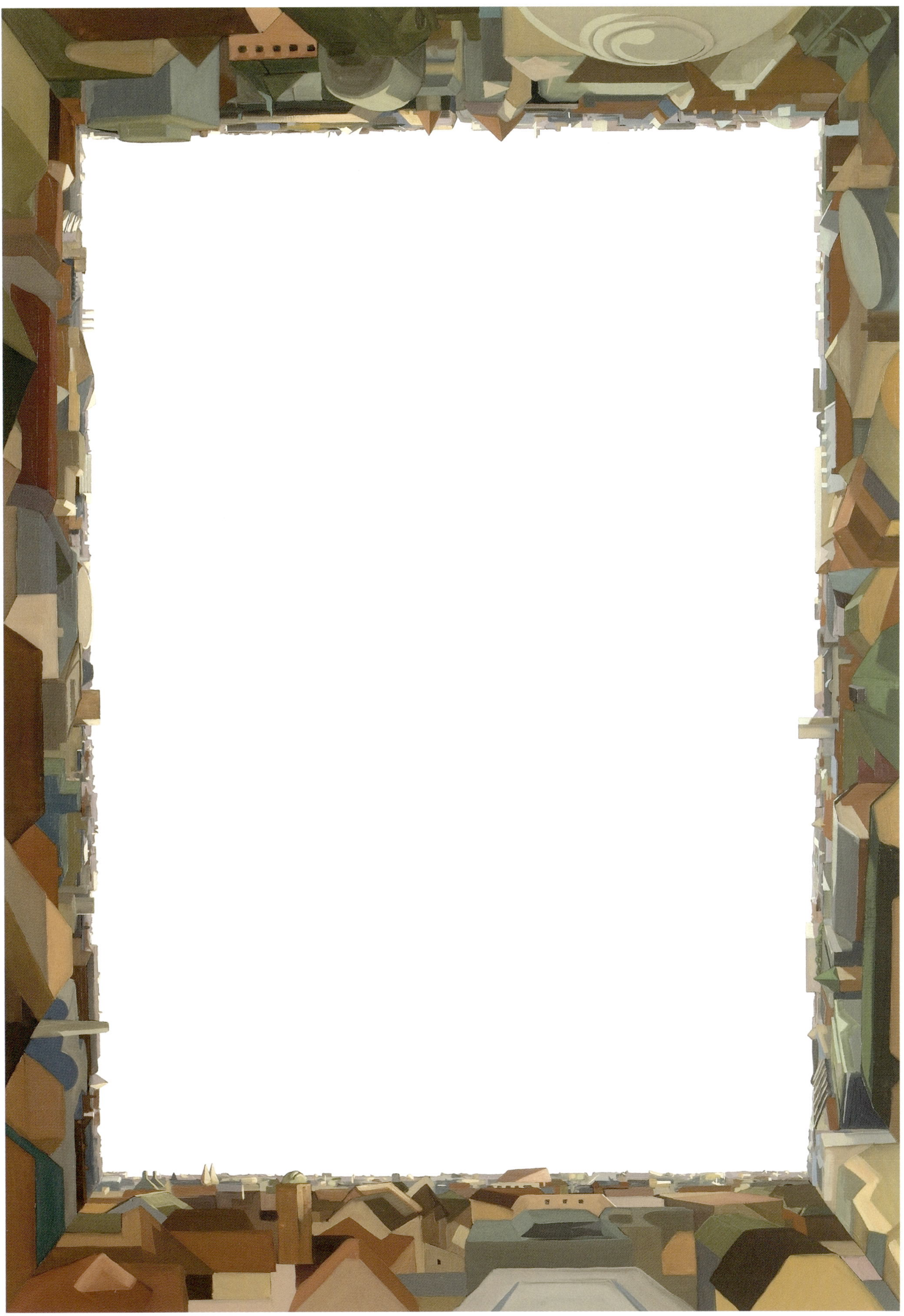

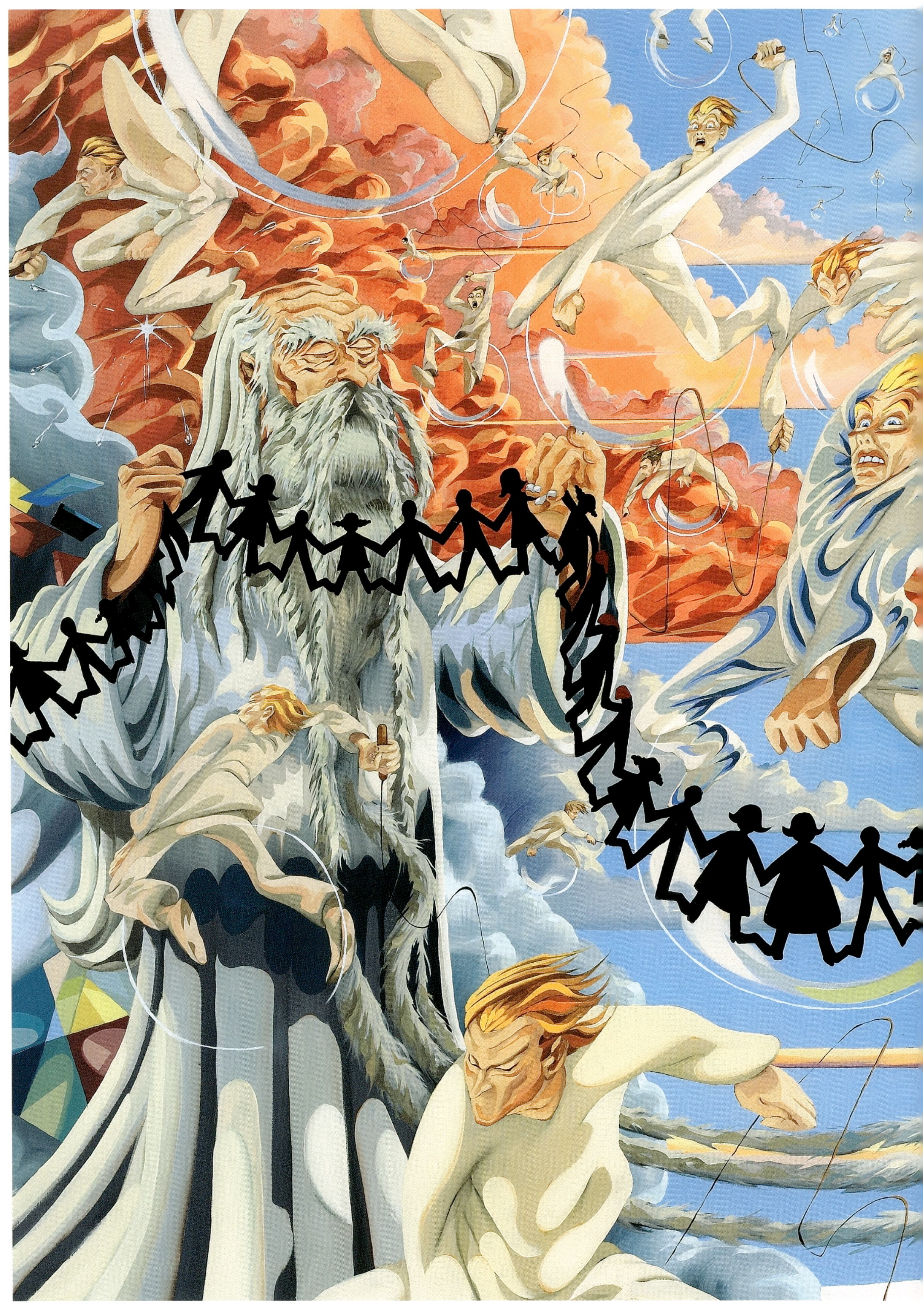

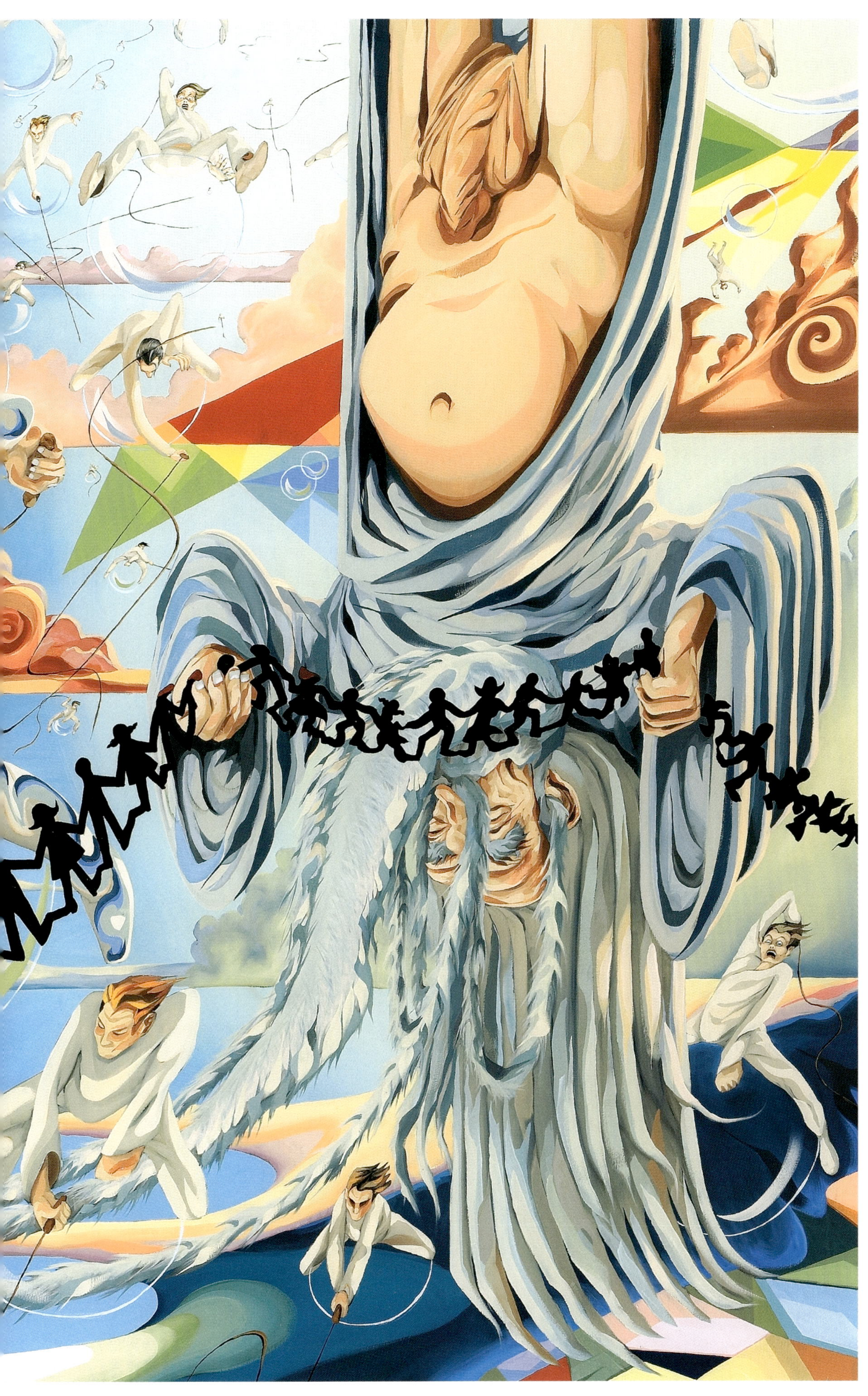

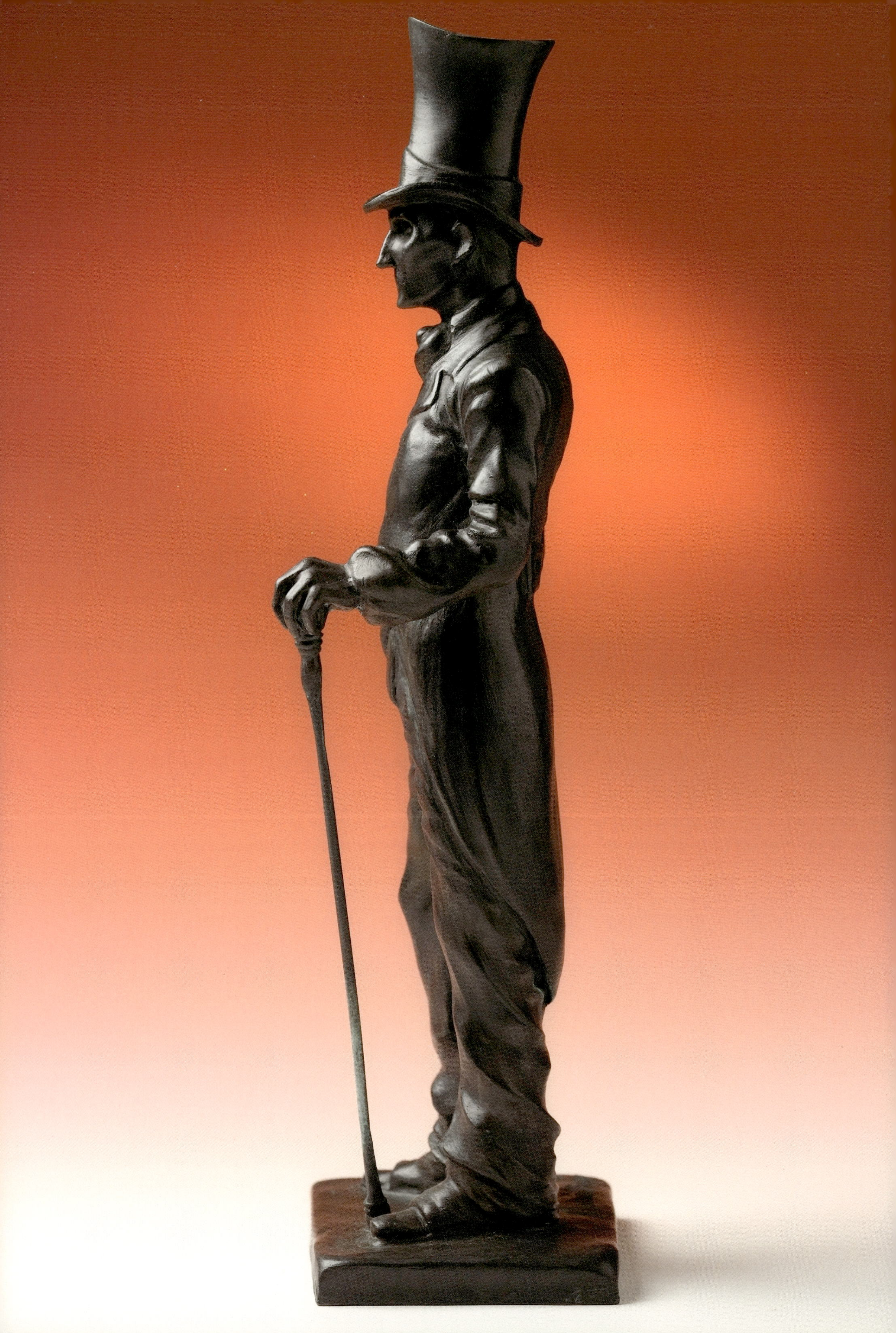

Martin Bigum

> Pictures embodying something (rather than of something)
> — P.M. Hornung

1. Inside every painting is a kind of *now*, a bull's eye, which must be hit.
The now is when all sensation, conscious as well as subconscious, con-
verges in one spot, and form and content coincide. A dynamic shape, that
I could not have predicted, is created in this unity, and unfolds as the
painting reaches its full potential, like a giant jigsaw, once completed.

At that point I am simultaneously the originator of it all, and completely
eradicated. It is in these few seconds of supreme joy that I think I see
the Face of God: fragments of a larger whole.

2. When I was a child and couldn't sleep, I would listen to the particular
sound that came from the darkness. It was like a creaky sound from
a large space, maybe the universe. Like an old creaky ship that quietly
turns in the night. But I knew what it was: it was the Face of God, a
heavy orb suspended and turning on its own axis, while all conceivable
mimicry flashed like lightning across its face. God's Face went through
all the mimicry in the world, as if looking for the right expression.

If I had turned on my flashlight and pointed its beam at the orb, I would
have seen something like what you see when you take the lid off a full
eel trap.

Or so I imagine.

3. When I was a child I thought that the best paintings and the best
caricatures that I saw were exact reproductions of reality. That whatever
was depicted was reproduced as it looked. I thought that what you
saw was the simple and sincere shape of reality and mind, respectively.
The soul, if you will, ablaze in oils on canvas or in the decisive drawn
line; that the subject was a reality that painter or draughtsman had been
fortunate enough to see, experience, and able to depict—for those of
us less fortunate.

This was due to the fact that when I put pen to paper and started a
drawing, well, I thought I depicted reality accurately: I drew what I
saw. The subject was real and actual, it just needed execution. In other
words: I didn't think I *didn't* draw what I saw. It is only after I've become
an adult that I have been told that there is a formal displacement:
from sensory perception to reality to fiction to mimesis. That one thing
is reality, another is art miming reality.

Nonetheless I stake the claim that I am constantly painting, writing, and making works of art from what I see. These might be phantoms, illusions, and visions. That makes them no less real. They are the same idea of reality as what I saw.

Everything in this world is an idea of reality.

4. The Face of God: just for one moment to seize the world, the vision, the insight, be the one who pulls the strings; to look out through the eye-holes in the mask.

5. That which is caricatured is the extension of mimicry and perception.

6. I don't work on my art for fun, it is made in dead earnest. Even the most outrageous work from my hands has the exploration of reality and the perception of reality as its purpose. It is at heart an expression of criticism. It is an overpressure. It is a commute between repressed elements, private and collective fear.

7. *The blind angle of all dialectics*: the site of poetry.

Where the antithesis to day is not unequivocally night; where the antithesis to nature is not unequivocally culture; where you suspect that the Face of God has mimicry that goes with no known state of mind; where I realize that there is something that is *almost* impossible to show. But which I nonetheless give my idea of.

8. My time is grotesque, mimetically faint-hearted, and every meaning either empty or hysterical!

9. When the Wall fell in 1989 a feeling of freedom coursed through not only the Eastern bloc, but the Western world as well: a proper airing was possible, even in our free world, which so desperately needed new scores to play from. Furthermore, access to different media exploded: MTV, CNN, computers, and digitalization in general. Polarity went under, the decade of globalization and individualism was kick-started.

What better way to encompass this than a narrative cartoonish line—with all its abundance and elasticity (or at least that's how I saw it)? Irony—sister to caricature—was even to become the hallmark of the 1990s generation. The *Whatever*-generation.

In other words, my experience was that my line, my *manner*, from my caricatured drawings, was transferable to the canvas, and that I had a sort of painting that I hadn't quite seen before, in that way: Pop art with scope, with honesty as its foundation. For one thing, as mentioned above, the expression fitted the times, for another it seemed refreshing: the postmodern blind alleys could be thoroughly aired out. Art had congealed at this point. The point that it was dead was made again and again. Through my way of drawing I could imbue gravity with fun and thus treat topics that were usually very difficult to come to grips with.

10. Confront the myths with their mimicry. To see if they can keep a straight face; no, wait: to unmask them.

11. "You're painting yourself," my wife tells me, when she is standing in front of one of my completed paintings. "The subjects reflect your life and your thoughts. And everyone in there has your nose!" I don't see any of this myself (maybe apart from the bit about the nose). At that point I have been through a metamorphosis where what subconsciously occupies me has been objectified into artistic content and form. And the reason that I have had to resort to that exact expression is my inability to express the basic feeling with words or reason. Art comes into being as a last resort.

But about my painting myself: for many years I thought I was going to be an actor. Now I have to act with the components of the painting instead. The painting is my stage, my movie. As a painter, you are your own direc-tor: I produce stills from movies that were never made. The public has to supply what comes *before* my depiction, and what comes *after*. But most of all what is *implied* in my presentation. I am simultaneously the drama-tist, director, actor, set designer, prompter, and critic.

I realize that the canvases reflect the outer as well as the inner world. The basis of every subject is experiences that get their final realization— be it however diffuse or corny—in the final painting. There is an urge that controls all of this. Regarded logically and pragmatically it is non-existent.

11. Every painting is having been close enough to shake the Face of God.

12. Art history seems to agree that the mimetically satirical is to be found with Holbein, Bosch, Brueghel, Daumier, Hogarth, F.X. Messerschmidt, Lautrec, Hart Benton, Stanley Spencer, Barlak, Grosz, Dix, Magritte, Dali, Immendorf, Koons, and Hirst, among others.

When I see Rembrandt, Goya, Degas, Renoir, van Gogh, Gauguin, Munch, Klimt, Matisse, and Picasso (and so on), I nonetheless think: Why has no one pointed out the mimetic, satirical, ironic, caricatured, and even cartoonish in *their* art? In relation to their role models, they were certainly caricatured and "simplified."

Where is the demarcation line between "serious" painting and caricature? All the way out where word and descriptions cease? When does an artistic form become so dynamic that it becomes "humorous"? Some will say that the difference lies in whether you surrender to the indefinable. The pointless, the non-illustrative: that which lives in itself, and does not depend on didactics.

But for me there is a huge challenge in cloning these two fields: that which is regarded as "stupid" and "off-limits" is always interesting for an artist to confront.

Art history is not stable—it changes all the time.

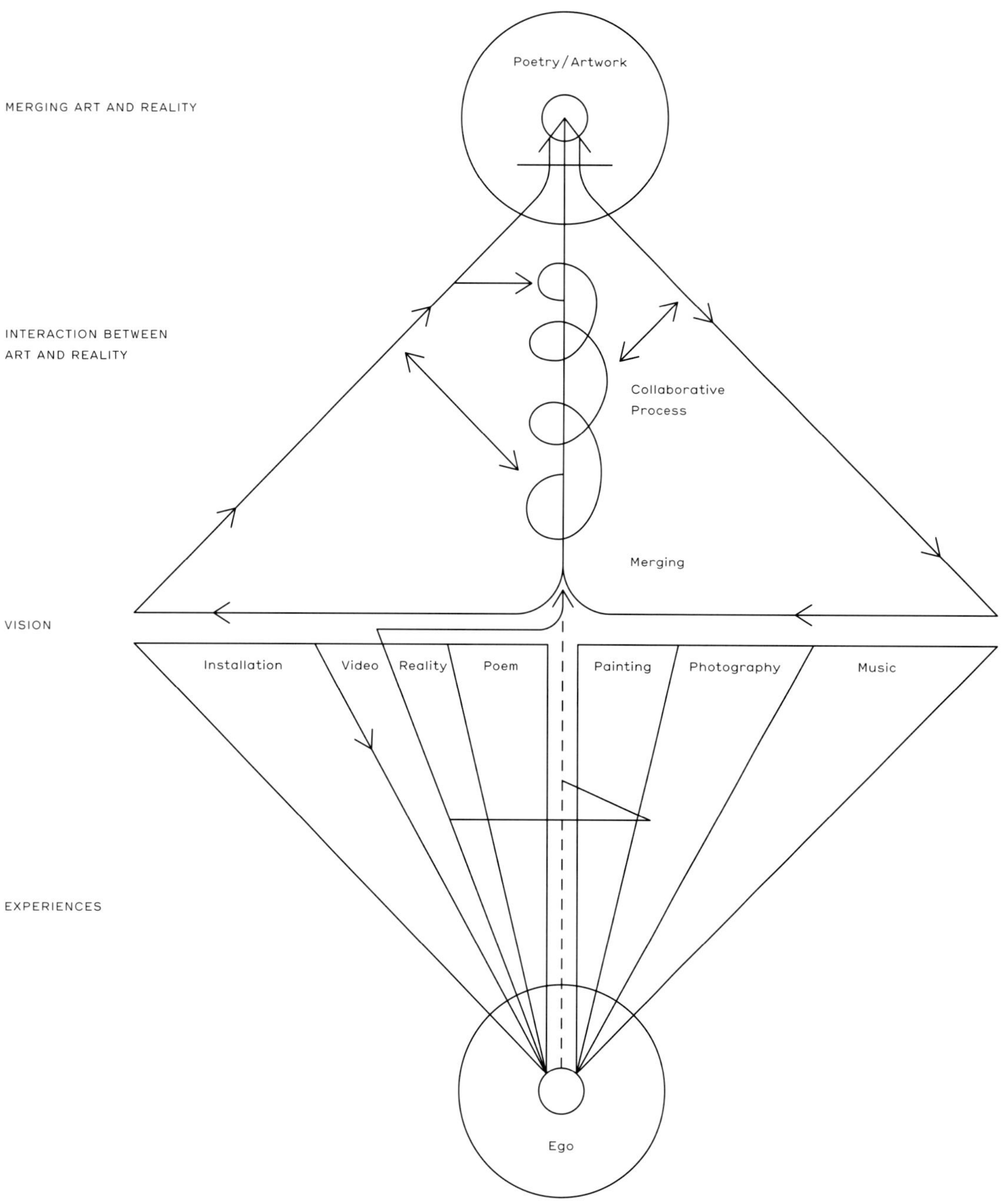
Poetry / Artwork
MERGING ART AND REALITY
INTERACTION BETWEEN
ART AND REALITY
Collaborative
Process
Merging
VISION
Installation
Video
Reality
Poem
Painting
Photography
Music
EXPERIENCES
Ego

All in all, it is my job as a pictorial artist to question everything in existence. Even art history.

13. The Mouth of Hell is in the Face of God.

14. Human mimicry, in all its variation, is different from person to person, from situation to situation. It undulates back and forth. Reaction engenders reaction; mimicry as waves on the human ocean, giving birth to new waves of mimicry.

One person's smile becomes another person's slack-jawed wonder, one person's listening becomes another person's sneer, one person's apathy becomes another person's question, one person's answer becomes another person's hushing, and one person's shout becomes another person's averted face. There is a great face out there in the dark that changes between beautiful and ugly, hot and cold, restful or sneering, disguised or self-absorbed, critical or radiant.

A baby's mimicry when it wonders, or screams, or just before it erupts in chuckling laughter; a child's mimicry, which often does not seem to reflect how much it *really* listens; a teenager's distanced mimicry, or the punch-drunk, the pure and simply devoted youthful exuberance at life. Or implacable mimicry.

Modern mimicry. Adult mimicry. Aging mimicry. The one that has forgotten childhood. That mimes society and accepted norms and boundaries. And when these are transgressed: When the person behind peeks out. What it looks like when you catch sight of the fact that we are all part of eternity.

15. I am not talking about the god of regimes or religions ...

Copenhagen, 2006

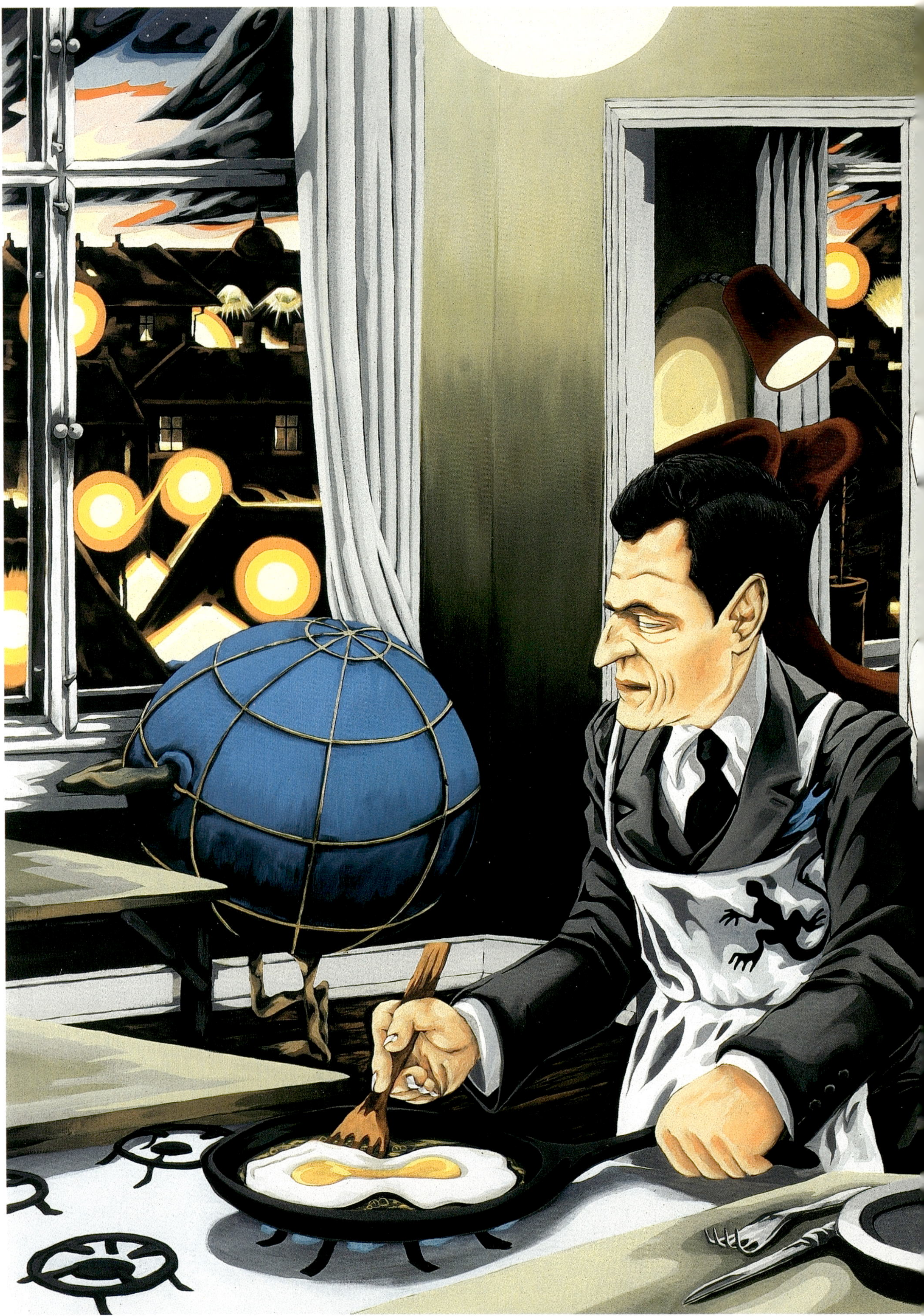

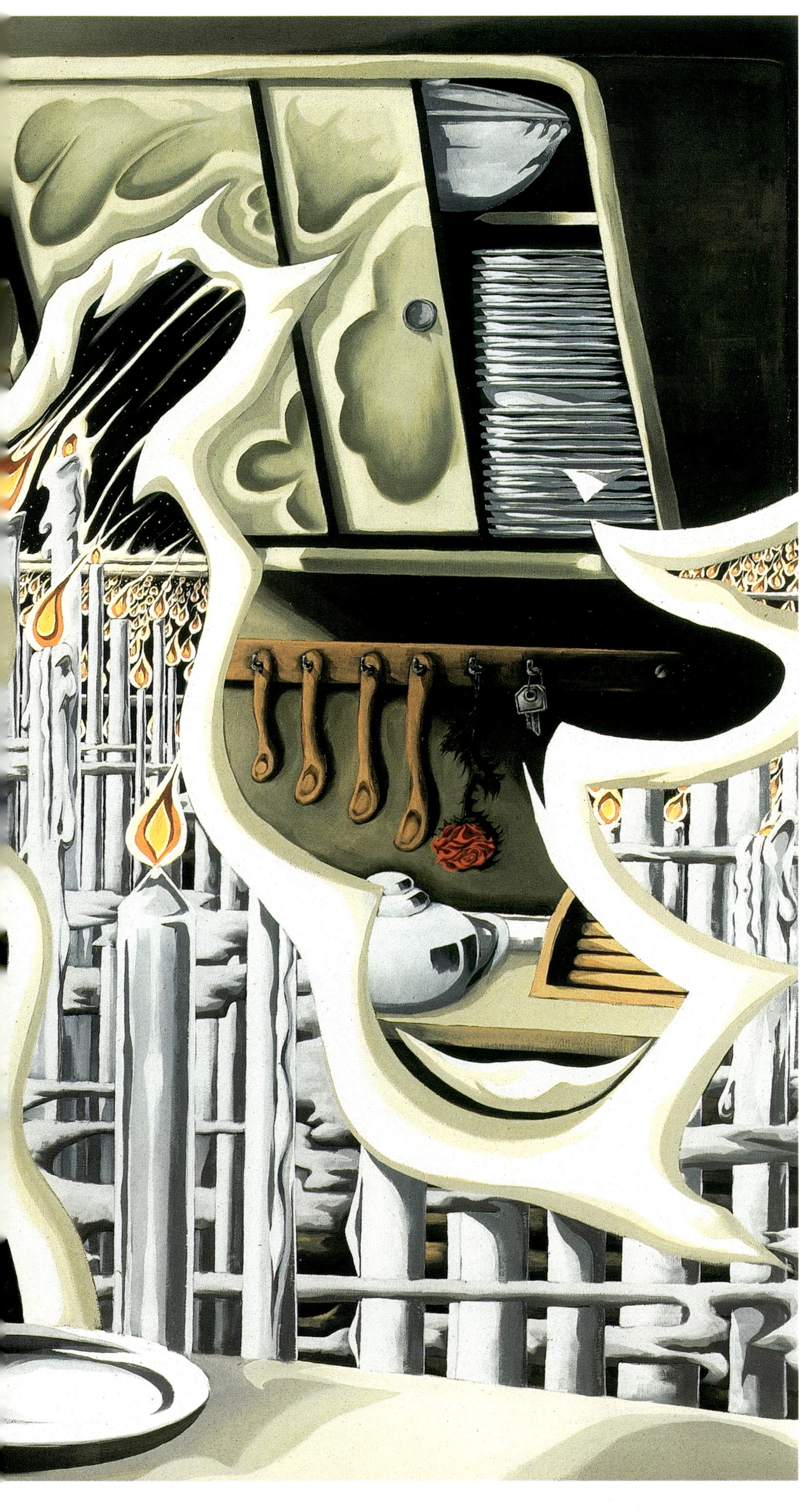

HYMNE (S. U. THOMSEN), 2003
←

HUNTER AND THE HUNTED, 2001
→

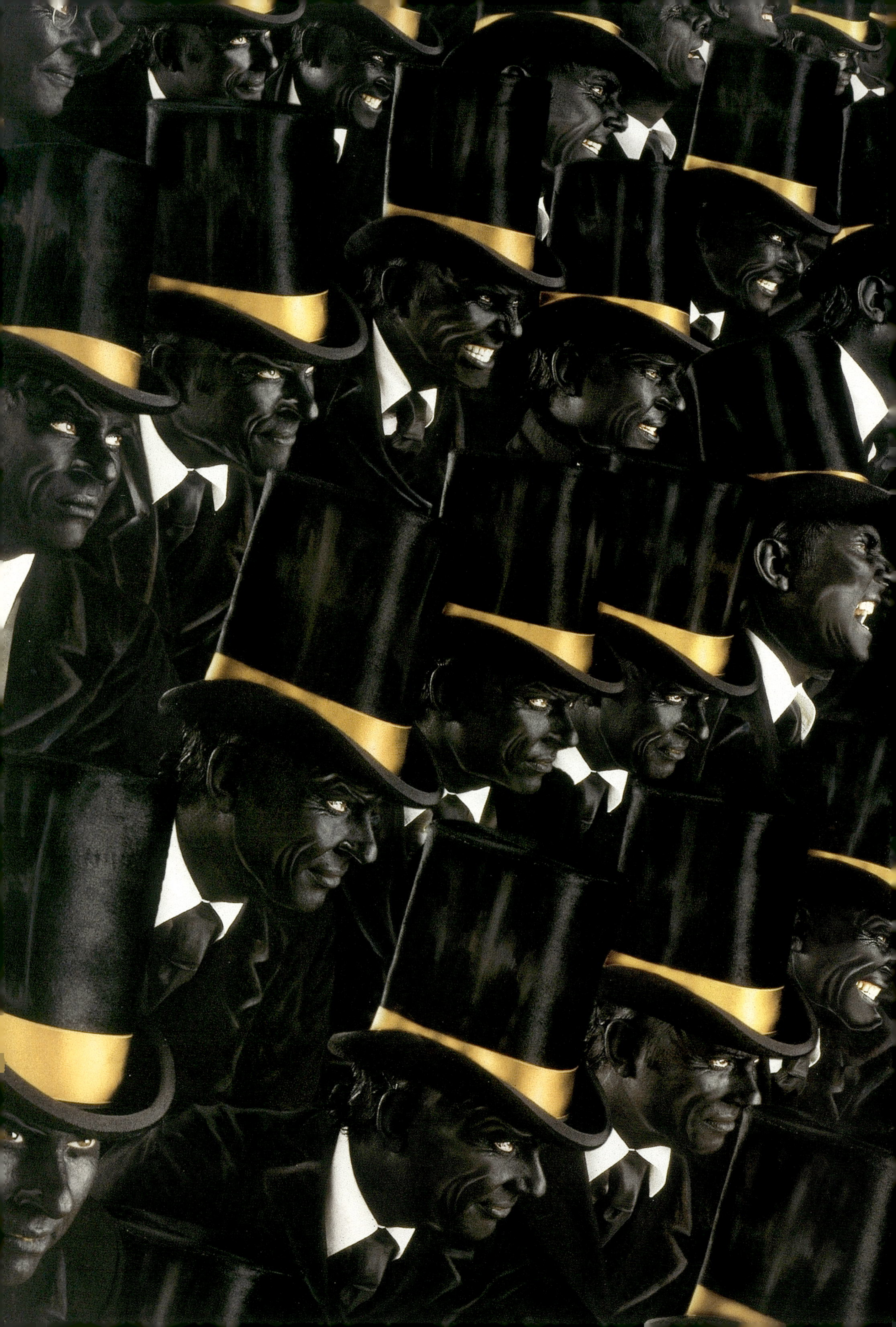

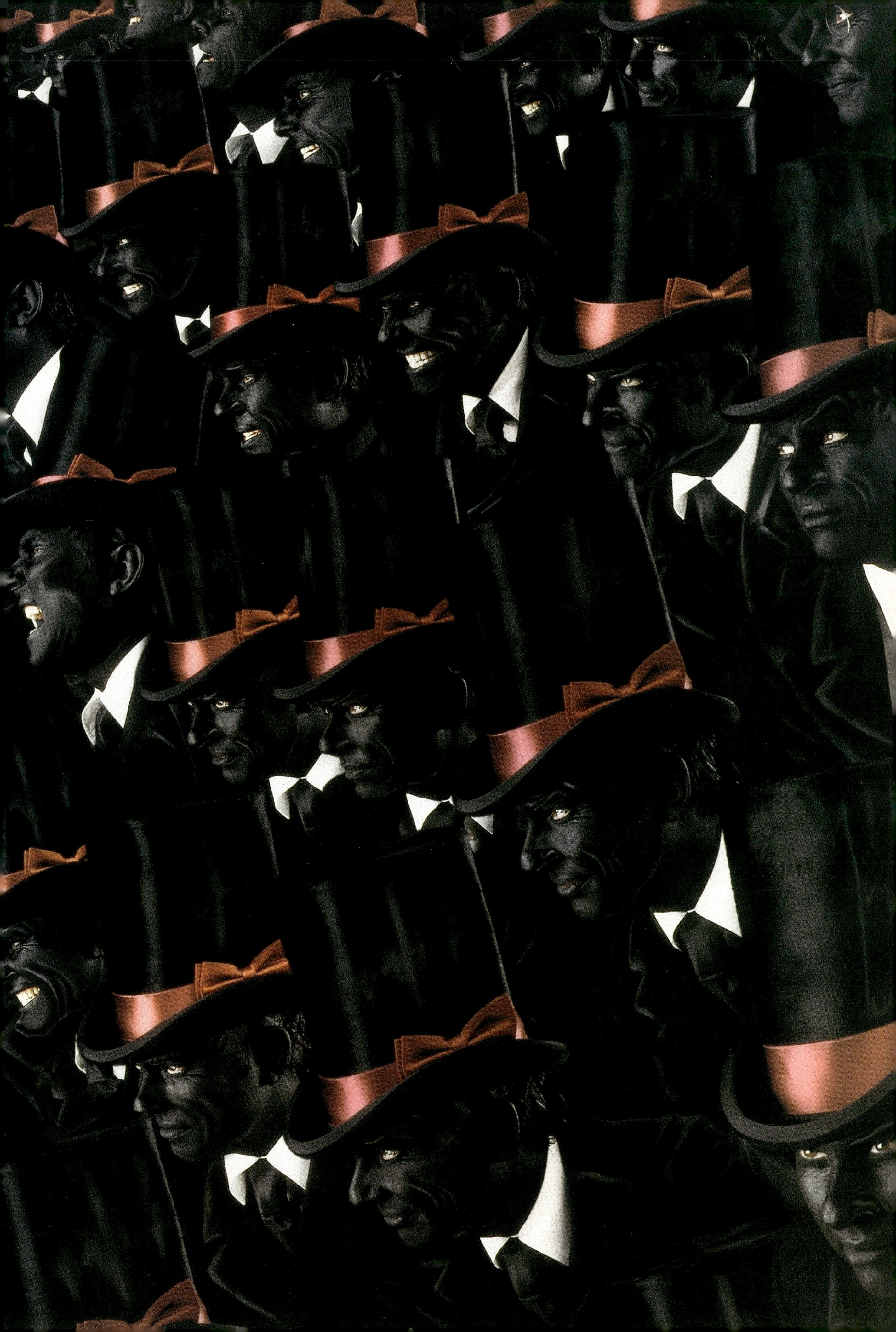

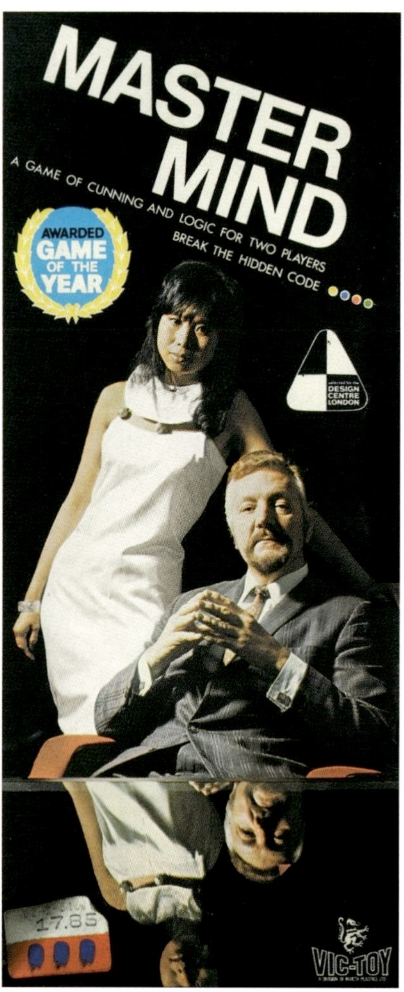
MASTER
MIND
A GAME OF CUNNING AND LOGIC FOR TWO PLAYERS
BREAK THE HIDDEN CODE
AWARDED
GAME
OF THE
YEAR
DESIGN
CENTRE
LONDON
17.85
VIC-TOY
A DIVISION OF INVICTA PLASTICS LTD

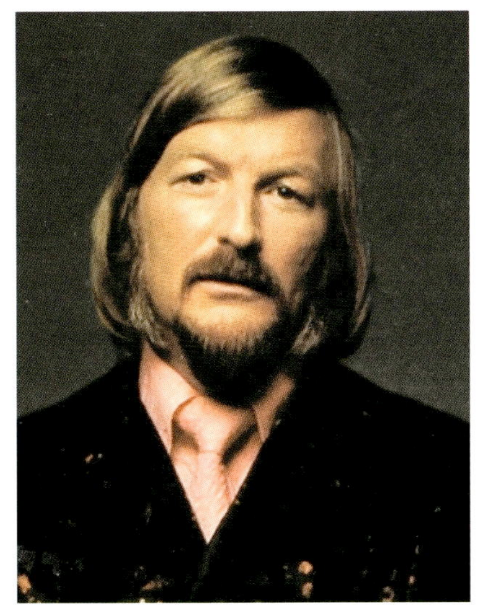
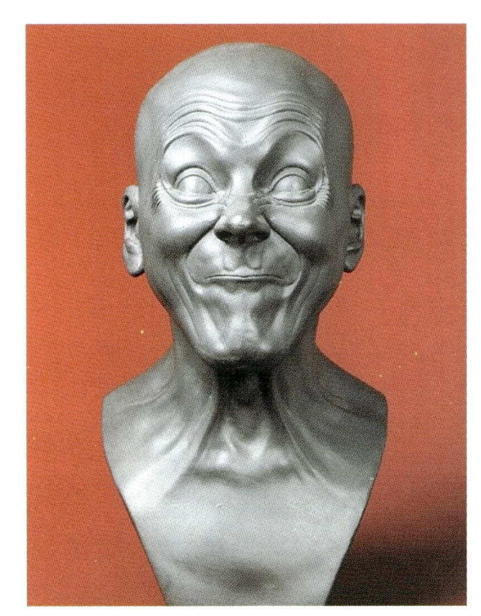
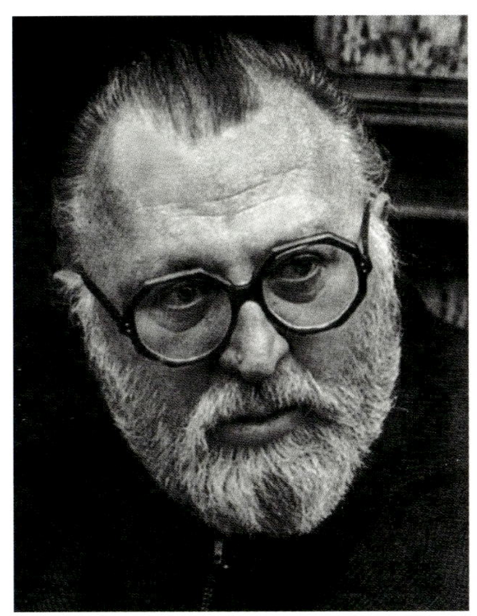
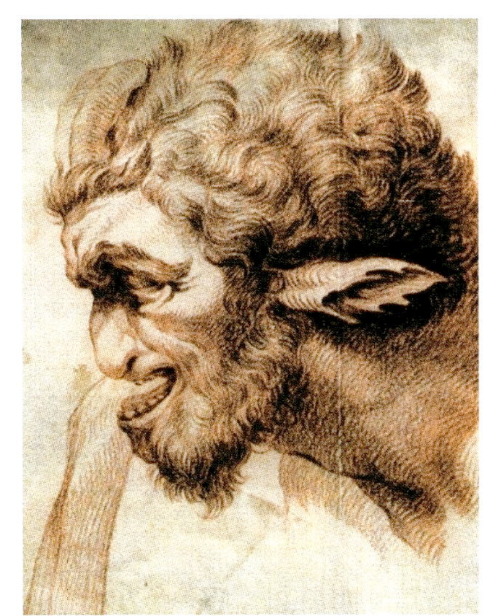
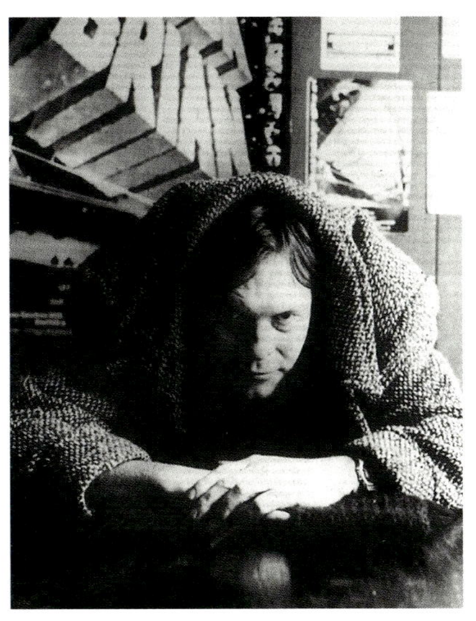
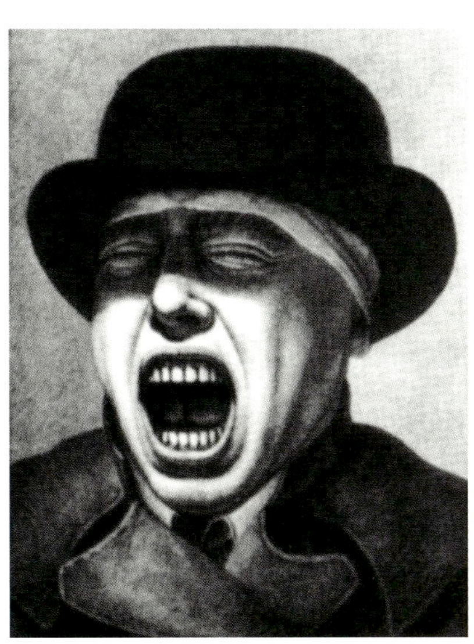

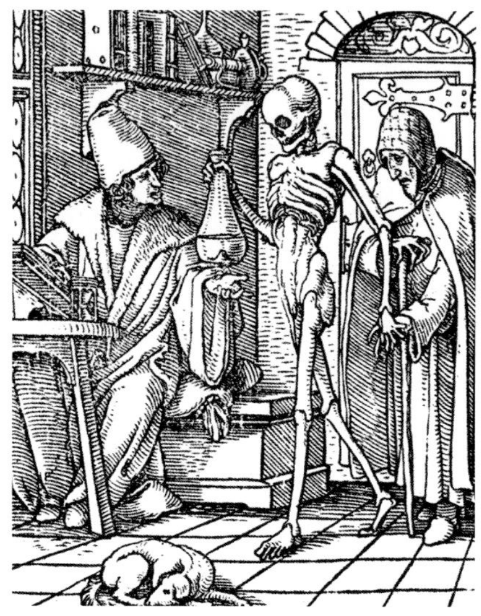

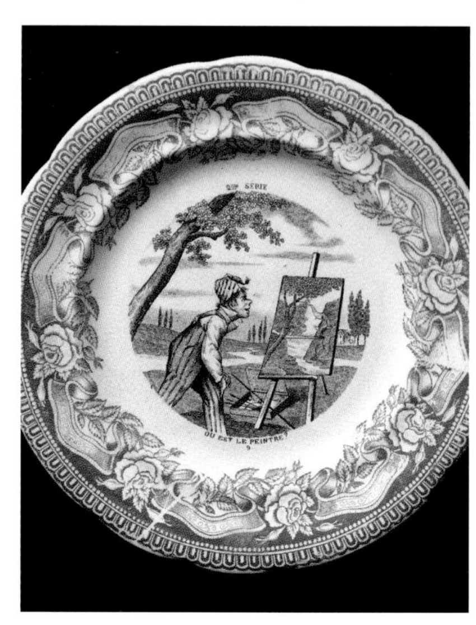

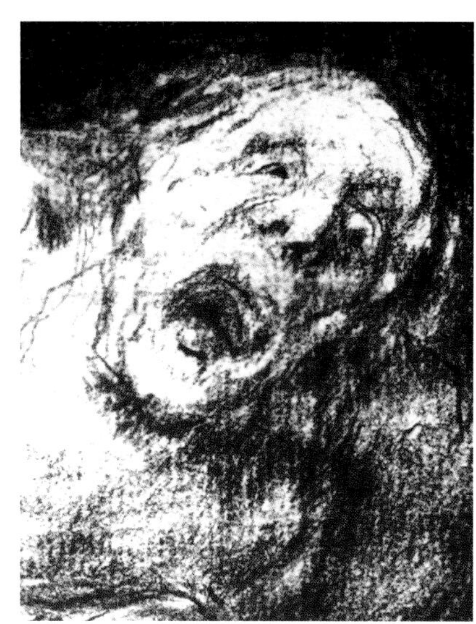

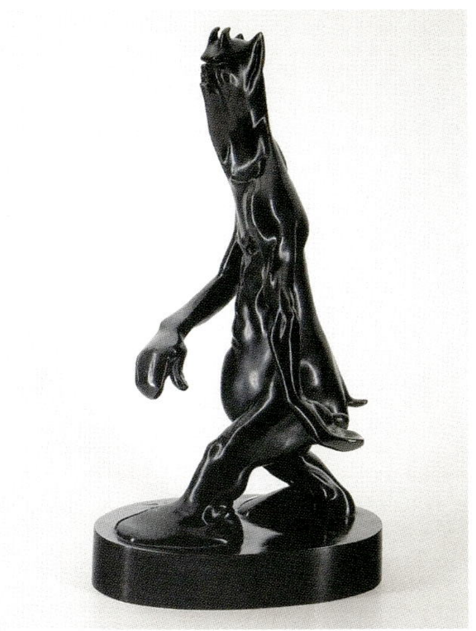

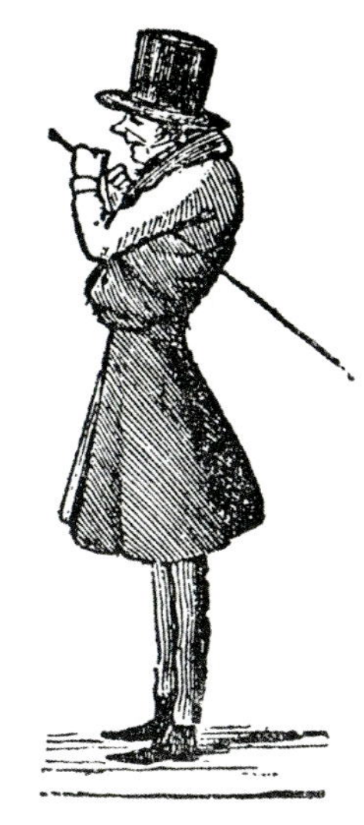

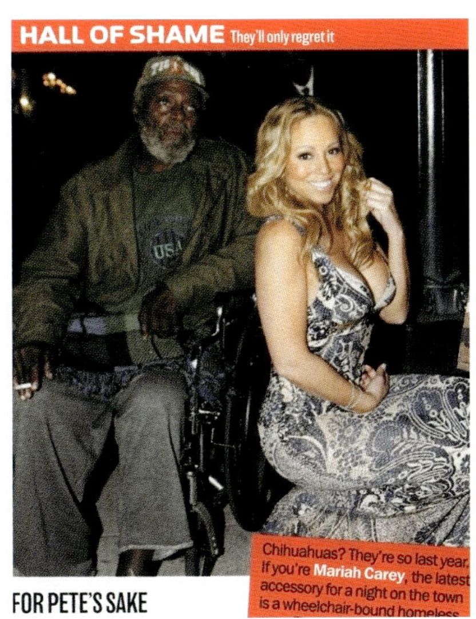
HALL OF SHAME They'll only regret it
USA
Chihuahuas? They're so last year.
If you're Mariah Carey, the latest
accessory for a night on the town
is a wheelchair-bound homeless
FOR PETE'S SAKE

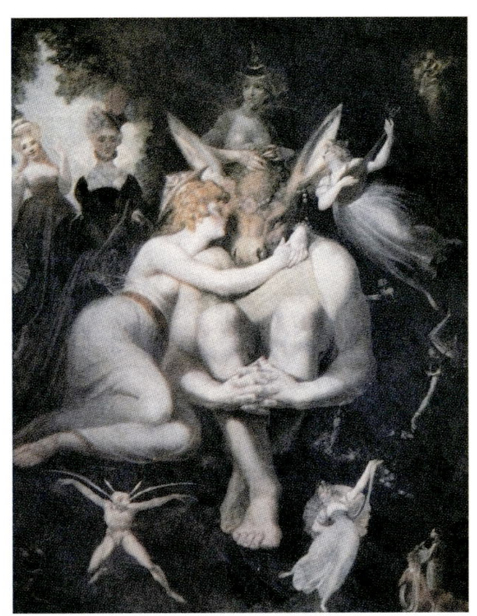

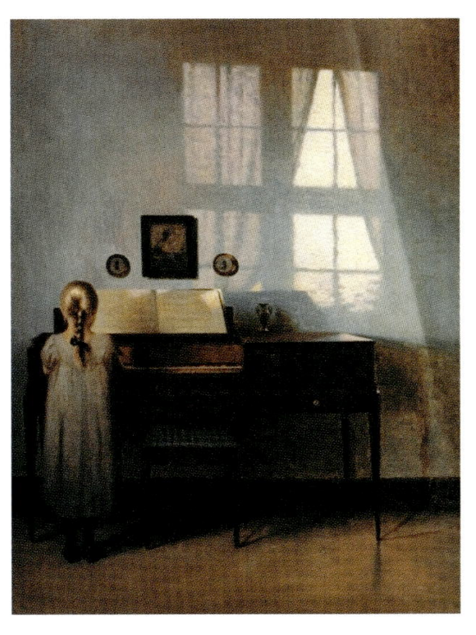

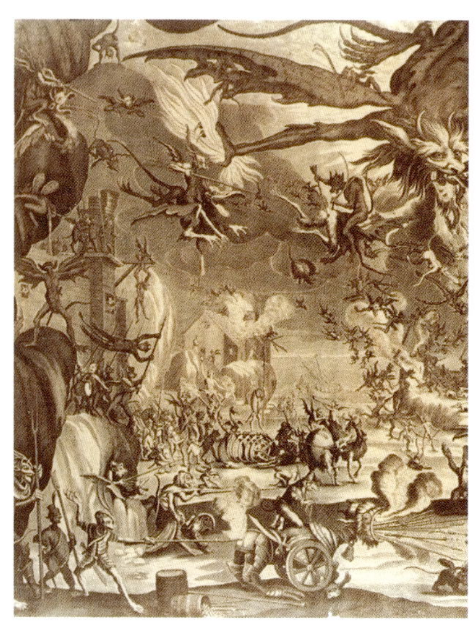

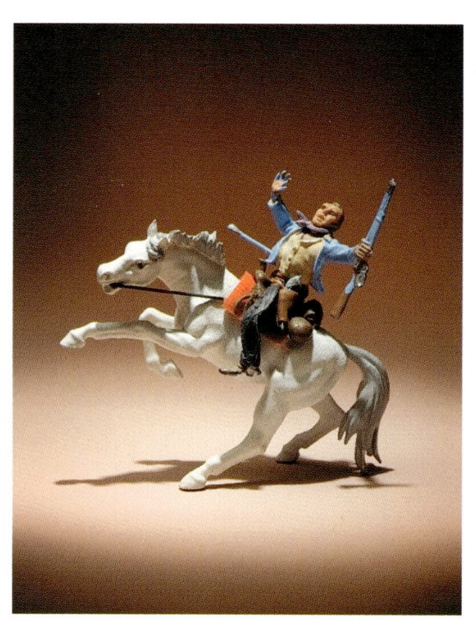

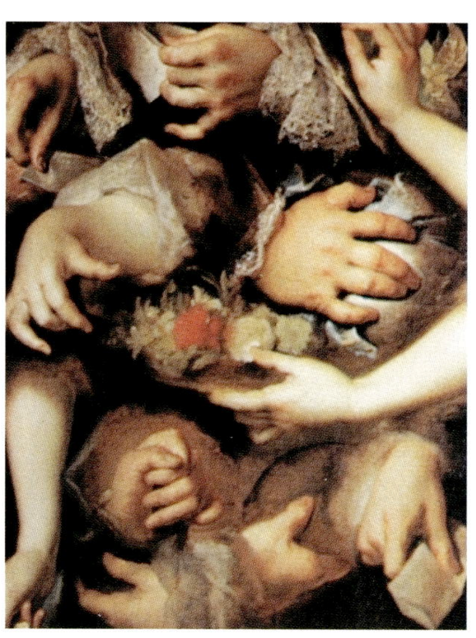

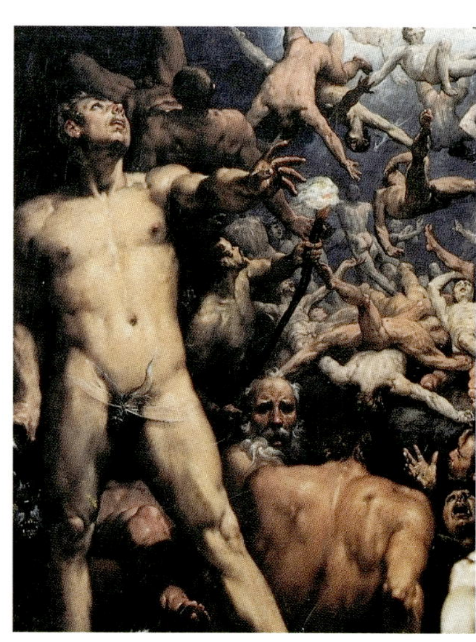

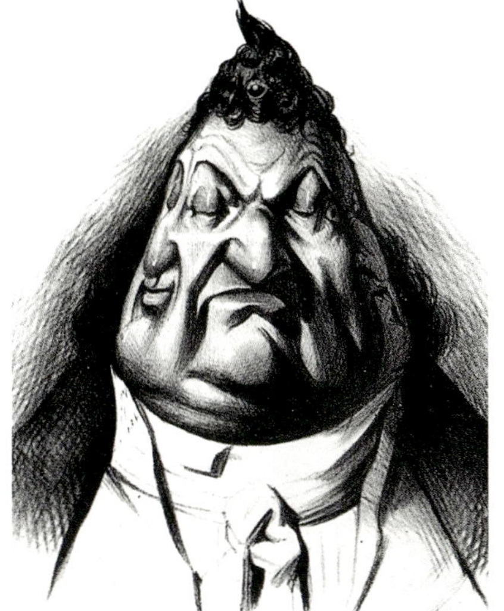

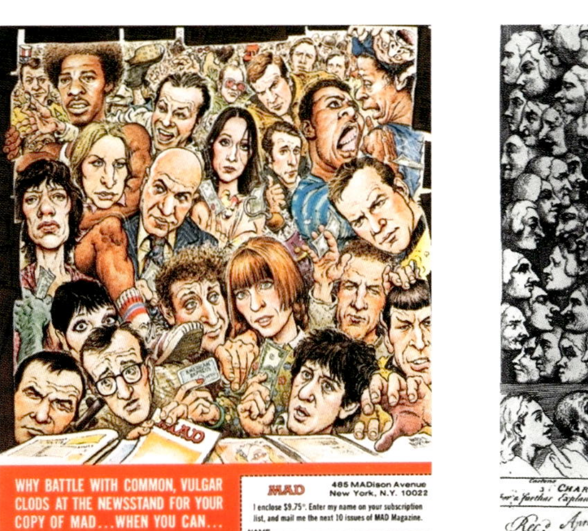

WHY BATTLE WITH COMMON, VULGAR CLODS AT THE NEWSSTAND FOR YOUR COPY OF MAD...WHEN YOU CAN...
SUBSCRIBE
...AND HAVE IT MAILED DIRECTLY
MAD
485 MADison Avenue
New York, N.Y. 10022
I enclose $9.75*. Enter my name on your subscription list, and mail me the next 10 issues of MAD Magazine.
NAME
ADDRESS
CITY
STATE
ZIP

INSTALLATION VIEW AT NILS STAERK CONTEMPORARY ART,
COPENHAGEN, 2005 [p. 4]
    LIMBO, 2005
    Oil on canvas, 190 x 135 cm
    Nils Stærk Contemporary Art
    VALE OF TEARS, 2005
    Oil on canvas, 180 x 220 cm
    Private collection, Switzerland

INSTALLATION VIEW AT BFAS BLONDEAU FINE ART SERVICES,
GENEVA, 2006 [p. 7]
    DISAPPOINTED MOTHERS, 2003
    Oil on canvas, 190 x 135 cm
    Private collection, Switzerland
    DISAPPOINTED GODS, 2002
    Oil on canvas, 190 x 135 cm
    Private collection, Switzerland
    RED RIGHT HAND, 2003
    Oil on canvas, 190 x 135 cm
    Private collection, Denmark
    FORMER TRAITORS, 2004
    Oil on canvas, 190 x 135 cm
    Private collection, Denmark

THE MOUTH OF HELL, 2005 [p. 8]
Wallpainting and eight paintings (oil on canvas)
Object: 102 x 104 x 17,5 cm; wall: dimensions variable
Private collection, Switzerland

INSTALLATION VIEW AT BFAS BLONDEAU FINE ART SERVICES,
GENEVA, 2006 [p. 10–11]
    VALE OF TEARS, 2005
    Oil on canvas, 180 x 220 cm
    Private collection, Switzerland
    THE GREAT DIVIDE, 2006
    Oil on canvas, 180 x 255 cm
    Private collection, Portugal
    FABULA, 1998–2005
    Photography, 100 x 70 cm
    Edition of 3
    PLIGHT, 1997–2005
    Photography, 75 x 100 cm
    Edition of 3
    THE SHADOW, 2005
    Bronze, 35 x 11 x 10.5 cm
    Edition of 15
    Nils Stærk Contemporary Art
    SACRED & PROFANE, 2003
    Oil on canvas, 175 x 300 cm
    Private collection, Switzerland

DISAPPOINTED GODS, 2002 [p. 15]
Oil on canvas, 190 x 135 cm
Private collection, Switzerland

DISAPPOINTED MOTHERS, 2003 [p. 16]
Oil on canvas, 190 x 135 cm
Private collection, Switzerland

TERRIFIED SURGEONS, 2003 [p. 17]
Oil on canvas, 190 x 135 cm
Private collection, France

SACRED & PROFANE, 2003 [p. 18–19]
Oil on canvas, 175 x 300 cm
Private collection, Switzerland

RED RIGHT HAND, 2003 [p. 21]
Oil on canvas, 190 x 135 cm
Private collection, Denmark

BITTER JUDGES, 2004 [p. 22]
Oil on canvas, 190 x 135 cm
Private collection, Switzerland

PRIESTS, 2004 [p. 23]
Oil on canvas, 190 x 135 cm
Private collection, Denmark

SWIFT BIRD, 2004 [p. 25]
Oil on canvas, 190 x 135 cm
Private collection, Switzerland

VISION & FACT, 2004–2005 [p. 27]
Wallpainting and eight paintings (oil on canvas)
Variable dimensions
Private collection, Denmark

JURY, 2005 [p. 28]
Oil on canvas,190 x 135 cm
Private collection, Switzerland

LIMBO, 2005 [p. 29]
Oil on canvas, 190 x 135 cm
Nils Stærk Contemporary Art

VALE OF TEARS, 2005 [p. 30–31]
Oil on canvas, 180 x 220 cm
Private collection, Switzerland

VISION QUEST, 2005 [p. 33]
Oil on canvas, 190 x 135 cm
Private collection, Spain

FORMER TRAITORS, 2004 [p. 35]
Oil on canvas, 190 x 135 cm
Private collection, Denmark

VANITY FAIR, 2005 [p. 37]
Oil on canvas, 190 x 135 cm
Frederick R. Weismann Foundation, Los Angeles

HOSPITAL VIEW, 2006 [p. 39]
Oil on canvas, 190 x 135 cm
Private collection, Switzerland

THE SHADOW, 2005 [p. 42]
Bronze, 35 x 11 x 10.5 cm
Edition of 15
Nils Stærk Contemporary Art

THE GREAT DIVIDE, 2006 [p. 40–41]
Oil on canvas, 180 x 255 cm
Private collection, Portugal

HYMNE (S. U. THOMSEN), 2003 [p. 48–49]
Oil on canvas, 180 x 230 cm
The Museum of National History
at Frederiksborg Castle, Denmark

HUNTER AND THE HUNTED, 2001 [p. 50–51]
Concept/Portrayed: Martin Bigum
Photography/Manipulation: Thomas Fryd, 70 x 130 cm
Edition of 10
Frank Cohen Collection, Manchester, UK

PORTRAIT OF MR. WILLIAM M. GAINES, FOUNDER AND
EDITOR OF MAD MAGAZINE (PHOTOGRAPHED IN HIS
MADISON AVENUE OFFICE, 1991), 1991–2005 [p. 64]
Photography, 100 x 75 cm
Edition of 3

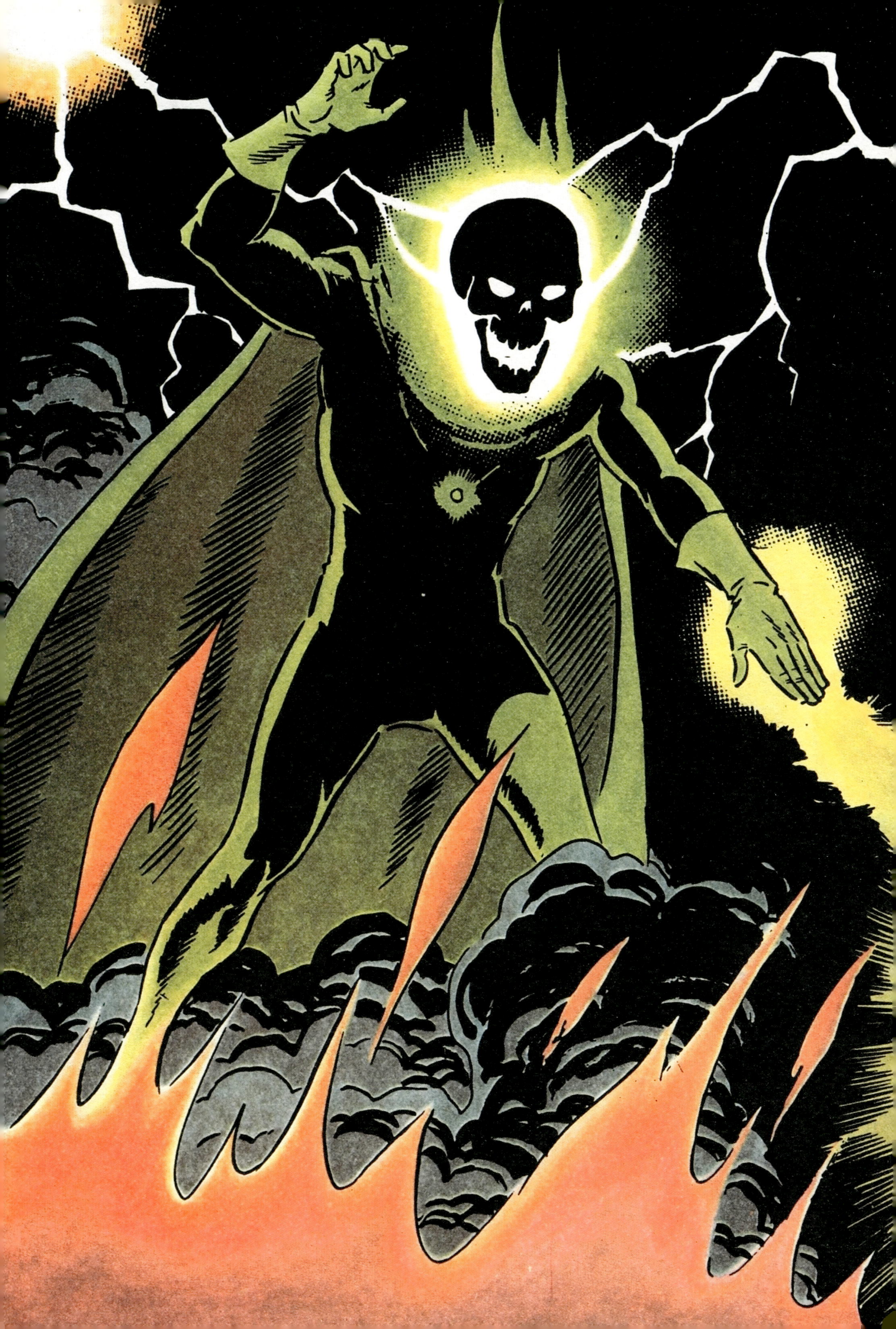

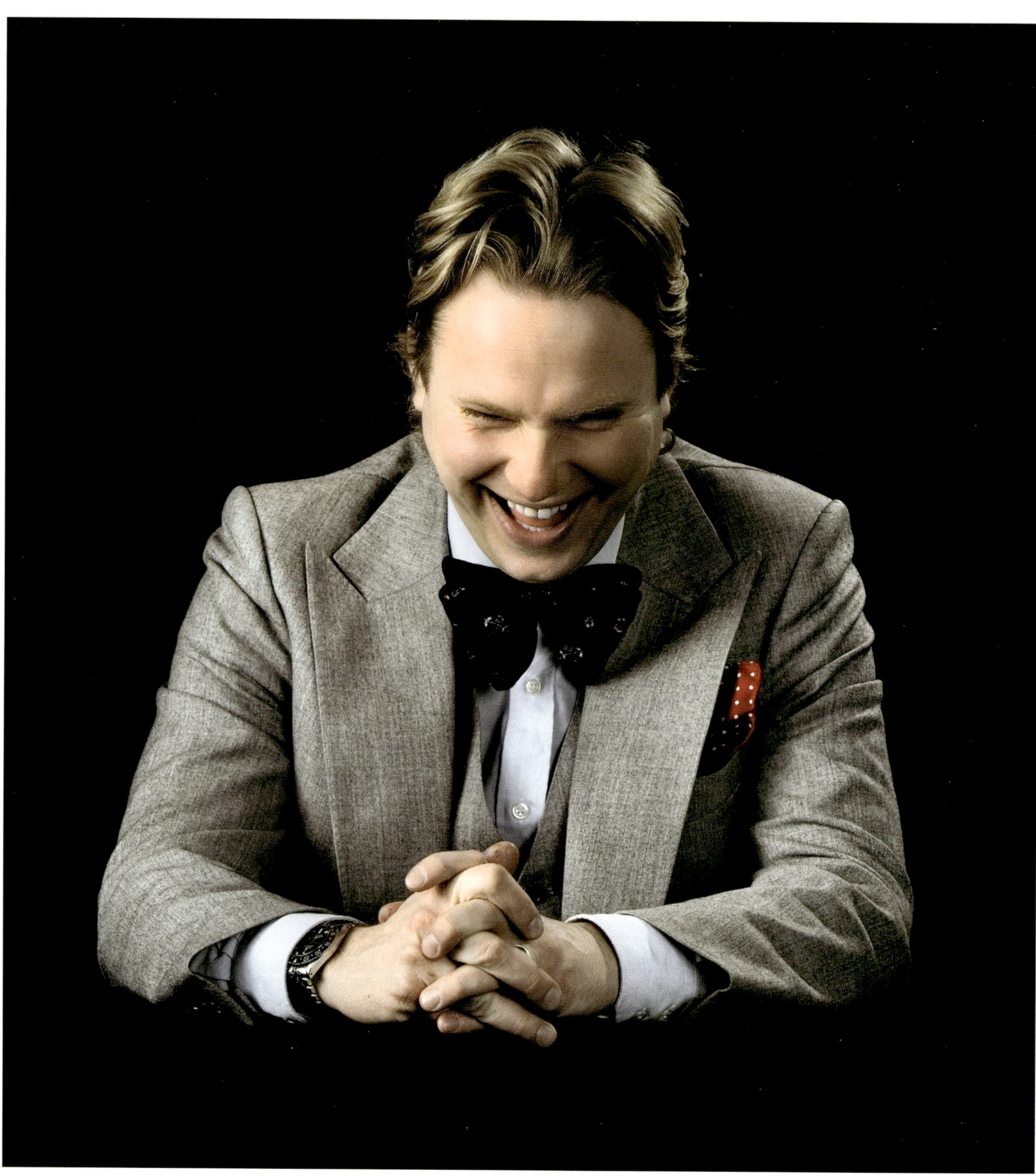

Born 1966 in Copenhagen, Denmark
Lives in Copenhagen, Denmark

SOLO EXHIBITIONS (SELECTED)
2007
I-20 Gallery, New York, USA
2006
The Face of God, BFAS Blondeau Fine Art Services SA, Geneva, CH
2005
The Face of God, Nils Stærk Contemporary Art, Copenhagen, DK
2003
The Face of God, Air de Paris, Paris, F
2002–2003
The Homecoming - or The World According to ART, touring: Malmö Artmuseum, S; Kjarvalstadir Museum, Reykjavik, ICE; Borås Artmuseum, S*
2002
The Homecoming - and Farewell to the '90s, a selection of sketches, Nils Stærk Contemporary Art, Copenhagen, DK
2000
The Notion of Tivoli + the album Overmorgen, Nils Stærk Contemporary Art, Copenhagen, DK
1997–1998
The Adventures of Art, touring: Kunsthallen Brandts Klædefabrik, Odense, DK; Herning Kunstmuseum, Herning, DK; Randers Kunstmuseum, Randers, DK; Portalen, Hundige, DK*
1997
Millennium, Århus Kunstmuseum, Århus, DK
1996
Millennium, Retinal Circus, Copenhagen, DK*
1995
Omen, Galleri Dalsgaard og Sørensen, Århus, DK
Devil's Own, Galerie Burkhard H. Eikelmann, Essen, D
Literary Body, Hole, Copenhagen, DK*
1994
Conjunction Theory (w/ Michael Brammer), Hole, Copenhagen, DK
Politikens Forhal, Copenhagen, DK
1993
Galerie Jespersen, Odense, DK
1992
Radical Myth, Galerie Stærk, Horsens, DK*
1991
Heartland, Galerie Pilou Asbæk, Copenhagen, DK

GROUP EXHIBITIONS (SELECTED)
2006
Faces, BFAS Blondeau Fine Art Services SA, Geneva, CH
2004
Hof & Huyser, Rotterdam, NL
2001
Painting and painting, Kristinehamns Konstmuseum, Kristinehamns, S
Danish Heroes, Koldinghus, Kolding, DK
The faces of King Alcohol, Rundetårn, Copenhagen, DK
2000
Carnegie Art Award 2000, touring: Konsthallen, Helsinki, FIN; Henie Onstad Kunstcenter, Oslo, N; Konstmuseet, Göteborg, S; Sophienholm, Lyngby, DK; Konstakademien, Stockholm, S; Listasafn Kópavogur, Reykjavik, ICE
1999
Drawing Show, Stalke Gallery, Copenhagen, DK
1998–1999
Eyes of Reality, touring: Nordens Hus, Reykjavik, ICE; Akureyri Kunstmuseum, ICE; 1999: Nordens Hus, Faroe Islands, FO; Horsens Kunstmuseum, Horsens, DK
1997
Cruising, Kunstforeningen Gammel Strand, Copenhagen, DK*
Arken's collection, Arken Museum of Modern Art, Ishøj, DK

1996
New Acquisitions, Århus Kunstmuseum, DK*
Face to face, touring: Brandts Klædefabrik, Odense, DK; Vestsjællands Kunstmuseum, Slagelse, DK; Øregaards Museum, DK*
Pictures of the city, Jyllands Posten's billboard campaign in Copenhagen, The Royal Museum of Fine Arts, Copenhagen, DK; Århus Kunstmuseum, Århus, DK
1995
Painting after painting, Kastrupgårdsamlingen, Kastrup, DK*
ART/OMI - International Artists Workshop, New York, USA
Vekseler Michaelsens Legat for Yngre Tegnere, National Gallery (Statens Museum for Kunst), Copenhagen, DK
1994
Social Video, Udstillingsstedet Nr. Farimagsgade, Copenhagen, DK

VIDEO
1997
Runner (Millennium), version 2, 14 min.
1996
Runner (Millennium), version 1, 12.5 min.
1994
Having it all ... Letting it go (Hybris & Nemesis), w/ Danmarks Radio, 5 min.
1993
Det bliver så tidligt sent, m. Per Kirkeby, Henrik Nordbrandt og Søren Ulrich Thomsen, collaboration w/ Steen Møller Rasmussen and Per Mannstaedt.

THEATRE
2003
The Threepenny Opera (w/ Pernille Egeskov), Betty Nansen Theatre, Frederiksberg, DK
1998
Jean Genie, Theatre 2 Productions w/ Lars Plumhoff, Trulle Jansberg and Jesper Binzer, Kaleidoskop Teatret, Copenhagen, DK; Vintapper Teatret, Odense, DK; MBT Scenen, Århus, DK

COLLECTIONS OF POEMS
2006
Poet-etik, Dark Horse Entertainment/Forlaget Rhodos
1999
The Veteran, Borgens Forlag, Valby, DK
1996
Overmorgen (Millennium), Borgens Forlag, Valby, DK
1992
Verdensvasen, Borgens Forlag, Valby, DK

MUSIC RELEASES
1999
Overmorgen, Epitone Records, DK

PUBLIC COLLECTIONS
Arken - Museum of Modern Art, Ishøj, DK
Artotheek den Haag, NL
Borås Konstmuseum, S
Frederiksborg Museet, DK
Herning Kunstmuseum, DK
Kastrupgårdsamlingen, DK
The Royal Museum of Fine Arts, Copenhagen, DK
Kunstindustrimuseet, Copenhagen, DK
Køge Skitsesamling, DK
Malmö Konstmuseum, S
Randers Kunstmuseum, DK
Silkeborg Kunstmuseum, DK
Skive Kunstmuseum, DK
Statens Kunstfond, DK
ARoS Kunstmuseum, DK

*catalogue

This book is published on occasion of the exhibition *The Face of God*, *Works 2002–2006* at BFAS Blondeau Fine Art Services, Geneva, March, 16–April 29, 2006, organized in collaboration with Nils Staerk Contemporary Art, Copenhagen.

EDITOR Lionel Bovier
EDITING AND PROOFREADING Clare Manchester
DESIGN Gavillet & Rust, Geneva
TYPEFACE Hermes (www.optimo.ch)
COVER *Terrified Surgeons*, 2003
PHOTO CREDITS Anders Sune Berg, Copenhagen
Didier Jordan, Geneva
PRODUCTION Musumeci S.p.A., Quart (Aosta)

ACKNOWLEDGEMENTS Martin Bigum would like to thank:
Marc Blondeau, Philippe Davet, Lionel Bovier, Florence
Bonnefous, Edouard Merino, Jesper N. Jørgensen, Nils
Stærk, Thomas Foldberg, Lars Malmborg, Jens Carl &
Merete Sanderhoff, Edition Copenhagen, Alexander Natas,
my wife Pernille, my daughters Miranda and Siska and all
the collectors who have been willing to lend their works to
the exhibition!

The publication has received generous support from:
The Danish Arts Council's Committee for Visual Arts and
The Danish Arts Council's Committee for International
Visual Art

Danish Arts Council

Nils Stærk Contemporary Art
Njalsgade 19C
D–2300 Copenhagen
T +45 3254 4562
www.nilsstaerk.dk

BFAS Blondeau Fine Art Services
5, rue de la Muse
CH–1205 Geneva
T +41 (0)22 544 95 95
F +41 (0)22 544 95 99
www.bfasblondeau.com

PUBLISHED BY
JRP|Ringier
Letzigraben 134
CH-8047 Zurich
T +41 (0) 43 311 27 50
F +41 (0) 43 311 27 51
www.jrp-ringier.com
info@jrp-ringier.com

ISBN 10: 3–905701–73–1
ISBN 13: 978–3–905701–73–9

JRP|Ringier books are available internationally at selected
bookstores and the following distribution partners:

SWITZERLAND
Buch 2000, AVA Verlagsauslieferung AG, Centralweg 16,
CH-8910 Affoltern a.A., buch2000@ava.ch, www.ava.ch

FRANCE
Les Presses du réel, 16 rue Quentin, F-21000 Dijon,
info@lespressesdureel.com, www.lespressesdureel.com

GERMANY AND AUSTRIA
Vice Versa Vertrieb, Immanuelkirchstrasse 12,
D-10405 Berlin, info@vice-versa-vertrieb.de,
www.vice-versa-vertrieb.de

UK
Art Data, 12 Bell Industrial Estate, 50 Cunnington Street,
London W4 5 HB, info@artdata.co.uk, www. artdata.co.uk

USA
D.A.P./Distributed Art Publishers, 155 Sixth Avenue,
2nd Floor, USA-New York, NY 10013, dap@dapinc.com,
www.artbook.com

OTHER COUNTRIES
IDEA Books, Nieuwe Herengracht 11, NL-1011 RK Amsterdam,
idea@ideabooks.nl, www. ideabooks.nl

For a list of our partner bookshops or for any general
questions, please contact JRP|Ringier directly at info@jrp-
ringier.com, or visit our homepage www.jrp-ringier.com for
further information about our program.

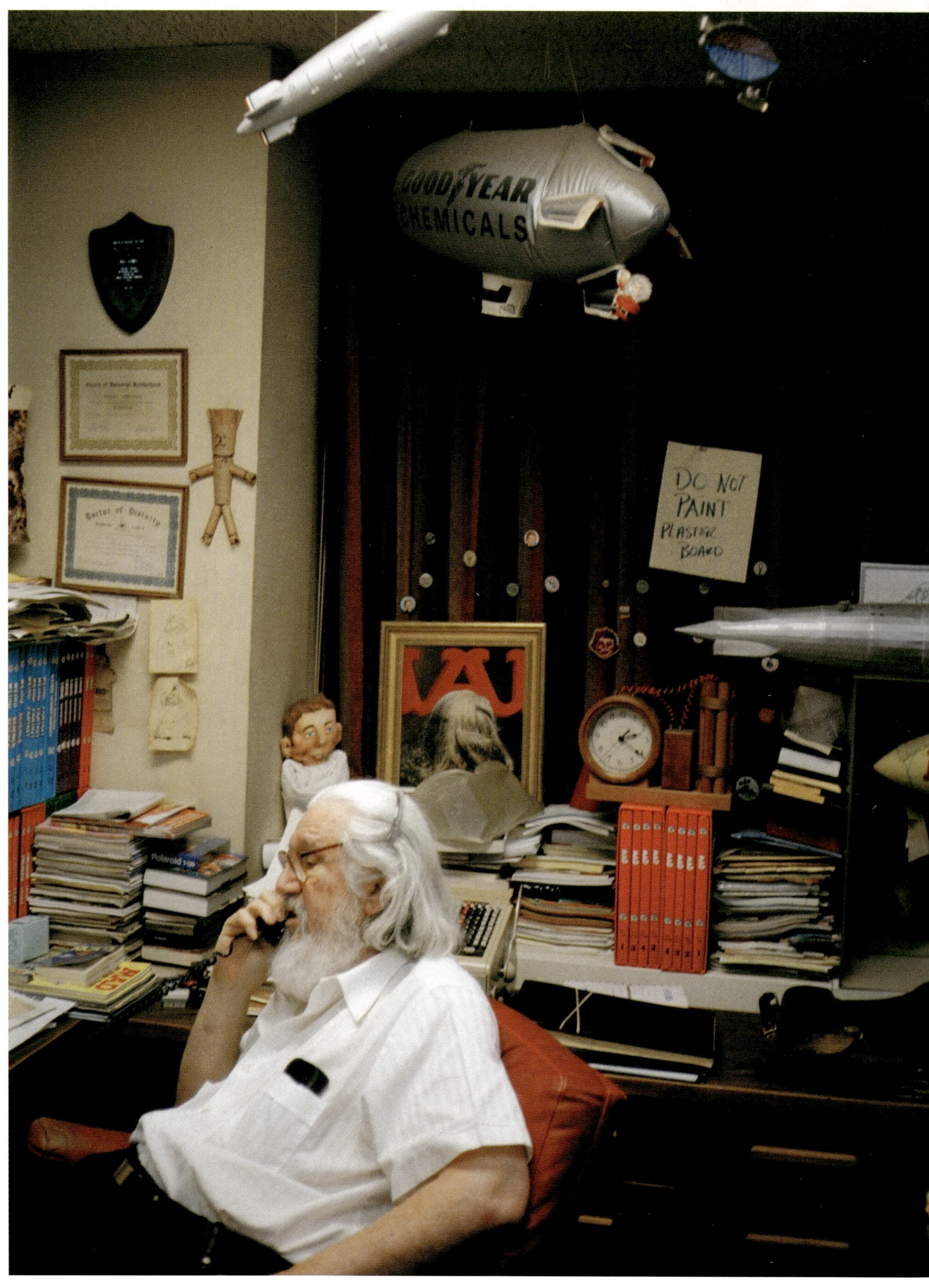

PORTRAIT OF MR. WILLIAM M. GAINES, FOUNDER AND EDITOR OF MAD MAGAZINE
(PHOTOGRAPHED IN HIS MADISON AVENUE OFFICE, 1991), 1991–2005

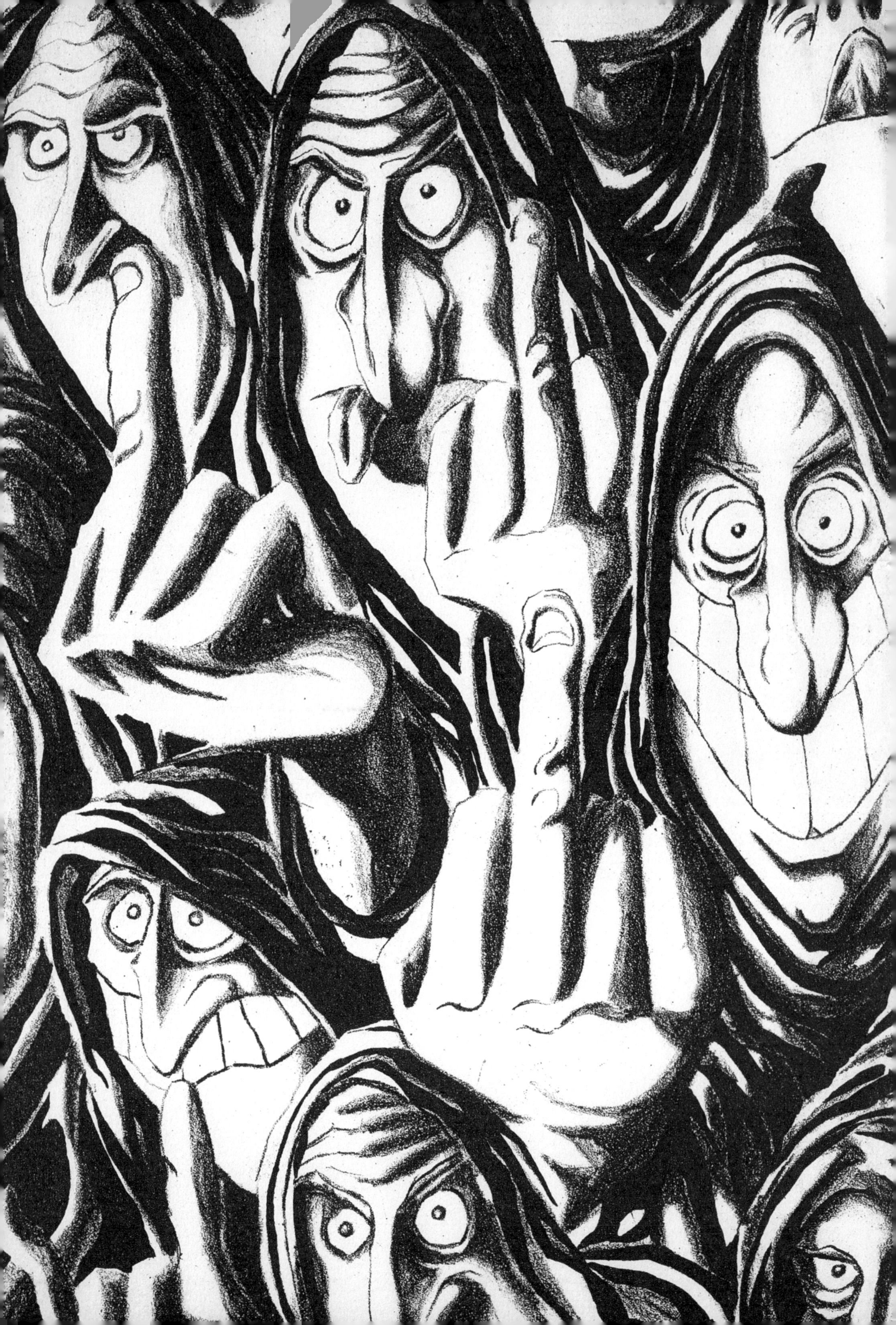